I invite you to be so gracious as to come with me to a "feast of the imagination": I promise not to give you any peace, rest, or tranquility; I promise to deceive you at every step; I promise to beguile you to such a degree that the most commonplace things will become mysterious, and in the end incomprehensible; I promise to lead you into every blind alley along the way; and finally, I promise to destroy all your hopes and illusions, to completely shatter everything you've ever learned in this life and all your accumulated Common Sense. Are you willing to take this risk?

Evgeny Kliuev—*Between Two Chairs*

The Power of Luck

A USER'S MANUAL

Dolokhov & Gurangov

Translated by Mark Havill, Ph.D.
Edited by Leonid Sharashkin, Ph.D.

DEEP SNOW PRESS
Ithaca • New York

Vladimir Dolokhov and Vadim Gurangov

The Power of Luck: A User's Manual

Translated from the Russian by Mark Havill
Edited by Leonid Sharashkin

ISBN: 978-0-9842873-2-1

Library of Congress Control Number: 2010924910

Printed on 100% post-consumer recycled paper.

Published by Deep Snow Press

To order all Deep Snow titles visit:
www.RingingCedars.com
Order Toll Free: +1 (800) 514 5011
Email: office@ringingcedars.com

Contents

Continued...

Translator's Preface

This past summer I once again found myself at a camp deep in the Russian wilderness, among the spruce trees and sparse, sandy meadows at the very top of the Gulf of Finland. I was there with my 13-year-old daughter, Sonia.

I wondered if *The Art of Soaring* wizards, Vadim Gurangov and Vladimir Dolokhov (a.k.a. Beard and Papa) would be there. They often appeared at these camps to teach classes and "work their magic." I was right in the middle of translating their second book, *The Power of Luck*, and it would have been great to connect again after many years.

The site of the gathering was incredibly beautiful, the weather was hot and sultry, and the water of the Gulf surprisingly warm to swim in. As we wandered around the camp the first day, we discovered a veritable village crowded with tents and tipis, cafes and tea houses, outdoor stages and big-top tents teeming with over two thousand Russians from all walks of life.

There were workshops and performances at every hour of the day and night—dancing, music, drumming, massage, spiritual practices, martial arts, healing, folk arts, drama, sports and games, and an effervescent children's program. Every evening I led Sufi practices late into the night, or rather through the misty twilight of the Russian White Nights, when the sun would dip down below the horizon in a dusky haze of pastel oranges and pinks, golds and reds, lavender and chartreuse— more colors than can be named or even imagined.

Late one night after my class, I heard drumming coming out of the forest. I followed the sound and found over a hundred people around a huge bonfire singing, dancing, drums beating wildly, so I sat down and joined in with my own drum. The energy picked up, the singing became louder, the drumming more frenzied. Suddenly, I noticed people moving in lines around the forest clearing, rapidly breathing a shallow, rhythmic breath, faster and faster. Someone was shoveling coals from the fire, laying them out to form a ten-foot-long "fire path." Then the chanters, feet bared, started walking over it, still breathing rapidly, rhythmically, stepping right on top of the hot coals, unaware of the burning fire beneath their feet. Even my sweet Sonia joined in, magically transformed by the energy of the group, not feeling a thing, her feet none the worse for their trip across the fiery coals...

When the drumming had died down, the dancers finally dispersed, an ephemeral mist crept over the waters of the Gulf. I wandered down to the shore, where the fire dancers spun and whirled, their pots of fire tracing mysterious runes in the enchanting early morning dawn.

There were classes in the art of soaring, too, taught here and there around the camp. You could always tell you were approaching one by the laughter—the irrepressible chuckles, giggles, guffaws, and belly laughs loudly rang out through the forest. There was no walking by, the joy was infectious. The workshops were led by magicians of all stripes who spun stories, taught powerfully silly rituals and games... and conjured miracles. At one of the classes, a woman was helping people fall into the water backwards from a tall rock while they exuberantly shouted out absurd affirmations. It was spectacular!

As it turned out, Papa and Beard did not manage to make it to camp this year—they were leading workshops far away in another part of this vast country. But they could definitely be felt in the people at the camp who had learned from their books and workshops how to soar high into the inner spheres of being, to that sweet place from which comes all success, health, harmony, and ineffable joy. That's where I look for them. *"I am a feather floating lightly on a gentle breeze, swirling and twirling, while quietly humming a child's melody."*

I have laughed and danced with Beard and Papa for nearly two decades. In that time, they have written nine books and taught hundreds of workshops throughout Russia and beyond. Their unique methods for changing life's circumstances through joyful affirmation, spontaneous dance, and seemingly absurd rituals has deeply enriched the experience of millions of people, helping them achieve their goals while making their lives much more fun in the process. I must say that I have shared quite a few belly laughs with them myself, and it has been an ongoing delight to translate their books. *"I am a mysterious luna moth flitting through the warm, nighttime air in search of a cool windowpane where my translator friend is burning the midnight oil."*

What I most love about *The Power of Luck* is its sense of theater. I often practice it with my children. They never know if I'm doing magic or just fooling around... or both. Sometimes I will claim credit for everyday events—the traffic light turning green exactly as I approach—while at other times I may utilize wild and absurd flourishes of verbal exuberance in order to deflect attention from the real magic being performed. The most important thing is to have fun! Not taking myself seriously. And to laugh. Yes, miracles can only happen while soaring on wings of hilarity and mirth.

I hope this day finds you sparkling of heart as you begin reading these tales of magical delight. May you find inspiration in the stories, so that you, too, can take off and soar into the heights of the inner world, realizing that you are the creator of your own destiny, no one else—only you can alter your life to discover abundance, joy, and peace. The time is now, the place is here, and YOU are the person behind the curtain.

"I am the dandelion puff blown apart by the summer breeze and dispersed into the world to plant new seeds of joy, laughter, and just plain silliness wherever I find the torpor of seriousness within me or... well, isn't everything within me, after all?"

Mark Havill, Ph.D.
Translator

About the Translator

Mark Havill has studied Russian for nearly five decades, culminating in his Ph.D. in Slavic Linguistics and Folklore from the University of Virginia. Since 1987 he has traveled to Russia seventeen times, teaching workshops in cities and at summer gatherings in the countryside. He has practiced conscious spiritual development for nearly forty years and is a senior teacher in the Sufi Ruhaniat International. He has known and worked with the authors since 1993.

Introduction

In the beginning was the pun.

Samuel Beckett—*Murphy*

In this second book, we continue our introduction to "magical" practices first revealed in the book *The Art of Soaring*. This volume boasts an expanded theoretical section and a myriad of tantalizing real-life stories which will help "make the fairytale come true!"

From earliest times, Russians have been characterized as quick-witted, irrationally hopeful, and naturally lazy. We are raised on fairy tales, whose heroes are often ingenious loafers. Emelia the Fool, lounging on the stove, has his every wish granted with the simple spell: "By the will of the Pike, do as I like." While drinking in a tavern, Ivanushka, also a fool, manages to catch the humpbacked horse Konyok-Gorbunok and with its help seizes the Tsar's throne, winning the hand of Elena the Beautiful. The quick-witted and nimble cat, Kotofey Ivanych, hardly lifting a paw, becomes king of the forest animals and lives out his life in luxury.

The ability to act the fool and, not troubling yourself too overly much, to receive instantly all that you desire is a unique peculiarity of our national character. This is attested to even by the names of the heroes in fairytales—for example, Kuzma Skorobogaty, which means "Kuzma Quickrich." Irrational hope* is vividly portrayed in the tale *The Flying Ship*. An old man asks the fool:

"Do you know how to build a flying ship, so you can win the princess's hand in marriage?"

"No, not really."

"Then why are you going?"

"I haven't the slightest. Things just seem to work out!"

And, you know, it did work out well for him!

The unorthodox actions of fairytale heroes, their unusual behavior, often lead to fantastic rewards. In the tale *The Magic Ring*, Martynka, in reward for successfully completing a task, was given the choice between a bag of sand and a bag of silver. It is not difficult to guess that Martynka chose the bag of sand, which turned out to contain a magic ring which would grant any wish. When our plans are neither limited by a particular concrete result, nor do they depend on a reasonable amount of time to attain it, then the possible result will often exceed our wildest expectations.

The methods used in fairy tales to achieve results are extraordinarily simple. The ritual to materialize the flying ship, from the tale of the same name, is a masterpiece of fairytale magic:

"Walk up to the first tree you see, cross yourself three times, and strike it with an ax. Then fall to the ground face down and go to sleep. When you wake up, you will see the ship before you ready to go."

Foolish behavior, a belief in miracles, the habit of getting what they want "without coming down from the stove," and the sense of humor typical of these charming heroes of

---

* Russian: *avos'*—literally, "the axis of Creation." Reliance on *avos'*, while irrational, is not unintelligent. Rather, it is based on the intuitive understanding of the order of the Universe. [trans]

Russian folktales are the foundation of magical art as set forth in this book.

Reading standard esoteric literature may give the impression that magic can only be carried out with the help of objects of power, or by performing magical rites or spells. In our view, these are all secondary. The most important aspect of magic is that special state of being when you are charged with energy. In shamanism this state is reached by entering into a trance, often achieved through ritual dance and playing musical instruments like tambourines, drums, didgeridoos, flutes... Sometimes certain psychotropic substances are also utilized.

In traditional magic this state can be attained by observing a multitude of mysterious and unintelligible actions (rituals), whose details must be performed with strict exactness; any deviation could put the magician in mortal peril. As a rule, rituals are accompanied by ancient and powerful incantations secretly passed down by word of mouth from master to student.

In this book we propose a humorous, light-hearted approach to magic based on an extraordinary state of being we call *soaring*. Entry into this state occurs by various means—for example, by exaggerating problematic situations to outcomes which stretch the limits of absurdity, which cause the magician to laugh uproariously, or at least to smile, enabling the drama and seriousness of the issue to just fall away. It all becomes comical, and an unusual and creative way of embodying magic in life is revealed.

The principle foundation of our approach requires a healthy sense of humor, boldness of thought and action—perhaps a child's game—and sometimes even a bit of mischief. Magic is no longer a complex science full of peril, but instead it becomes light, harmless, and fully accessible to all.

Acknowledgments

This book, like the preceding one, was thoroughly edited by Liusia. She drew our attention to several obscure passages which were clarified, greatly enriching the theoretical section. Yura Samodurov proofread the theoretical section and also made many valuable comments.

We wish to express our deepest gratitude to all those magicians who have contributed stories to this book: Maat, Ilona, Natasha Lee, Zoya Krainova, Marianna, Olga Shnitser, Elena Yekaterinskaya, Galina Antonova, Olga Kiseleva, Mitrich, OK, Liuda Safonova, Tanya Gonova, Tanya Koroleva, Sasha Pugovkin, Galina Kurianova, Elena Savchenko, Irina Svetlikina, and Sveta Vladimirova.

Special thanks also go to Olga Mikhailovna Priambokanova, Peterpaul and Evgeny Kliuev, the Rottweiler Alba, Olga OK, Kolya Smirnov, Pavel Alimov, Petr Dmitriev, Richard Bendler and John Grinder, the film *Twelve Monkeys*, and the Lumière brothers who invented the cinema.

Some Theory For the Curious

For in and out, above, about, below,
'Tis nothing but a Magic Shadow-show,
Play'd in a Box whose Candle is the Sun,
Round which we Phantom Figures come and go.
Omar Khayyam—*Rubaiyat*

Imagine yourself in a crowded, stuffy room. Every-where people are sitting on old, dilapidated chairs, on rickety stools, on packs—wherever they can. Some who are quick try to occupy two chairs at the same time, or to snatch seats away from others. This is like the world we live in. But at the same time, each of us also pos-sesses our own personal throne, enormous, magnificent, rising high above everything in this world, even above everything in all other worlds. This throne is truly grand and majestic. Nothing is impossible for the person who ascends to it, and, even more important, it is wholly le-gitimate. It is the lawful right of each person. But to ascend this throne is nearly impossible, since it stands in a place which does not exist... It is nowhere.
Victor Pelevin—*Chapaev and Emptiness*

The Art of Soaring

Suddenly it dawned on him:
"Wait!" he shouted. "That was flying! We were flying!"
The Hermit nodded.
"I know," he said. "The truth is simpler than you can imagine."

Victor Pelevin—*Hermit and Six-Toes*

Have you ever watched how a bird soars on the wind? How it spreads its wings and glides easily through the air? Nothing hinders its flight. Merging with the elements, it becomes one with them. It flies effortlessly, sailing endlessly through the blue sky.

Soaring is one of the principal concepts of the system for practical magic described in this book. It is exceedingly difficult to describe this state of soaring in words, because it is a subjective inner experience for each person. While soaring, it never even enters your mind to attempt to name or define what you arc feeling, and the circumstances of life which enable one person to soar may mean nothing to another. Only through metaphor is it possible to express this feeling, as in the following story.

When I was a young boy, I learned to ride a bicycle. At first it was very difficult to maintain my balance. Each time I started out, my bicycle, seemingly bewitched, again and again toppled over, and I crashed down hard onto the pavement, scratched and bruised.

At last, though, I finally managed to "catch" that feeling of balance and, desperately swerving from side to side, I set off. Gradually I was able to steady myself and felt my dark blue "Mustang" become subservient to my will. I merged with the bicycle and, peddling effortlessly, I rode forward. The entire world around me—the gray pavement of the street and the long shadows of the setting sun, the lilac bushes and the hollow old pear tree, the chirping of the birds and the gentle summer breeze—everything took on an altered and elusive meaning. I can't explain this feeling, but in this new world my every wish was granted. Each moment was unique and absorbed me entirely.

You can sink into a very powerful state of soaring through spiritual dance (Dances of Universal Peace). Following is a brief description of the authors' impressions of one such evening of dancing.

Taking hands and forming a large circle, we sing an intricate song in an ancient language, accompanied by guitar and drum. With quickening tempo, our feet trace the beautiful pattern of the "grapevine step." Each person moves in syncopation with two other dancers—the partner and corner— first facing one, then the other. In the second part of the dance, the dancers, whirling rapidly, exchange places with their partner, face a new partner, and the dance is begun anew.

Combining a song in a powerful, ancient language with beautiful movements of the body, as joyful faces flash constantly before your eyes, brings you into a state of soaring. An energy of amazing force swirls around the hall. The eyes of the dancers sparkle brightly, smiles shine on faces, and the atmosphere is electrified by a powerful discharge of happiness and universal love. The mood and strength of purpose fills each dancer with ecstasy.

An exuberant Russian dance "Oy, How Good It Is!" is the highlight of the program; we dance it with wild abandon. It is interesting to observe the beginners—how their faces are gradually changing, how their eyes begin to shine with love and joy.

An especially deep state of consciousness is reached when we do a slow, meditative dance. Singing a simple melody, we move to a slow and easy rhythm, bowing slightly to the right, to the left, rocking forward and backward, like rowing a boat, sinking gradually into vast depths of inner bliss.

We feel a warm glow in the center of our breast; a gentle, pleasant fire flares up within us, crackling steadily like birch logs blazing in a well-stoked Russian woodstove. Our hearts expand to encompass the entire hall, merging with the other dancers, pulsating in time with the movements, the singing.

We become one with the circle; we are both the observer and the observed; everyone sings through us, and we sing through everyone. Who is it that moves us? Who sings with our voice? Where have space and time disappeared to? These questions hang in the atmosphere.

The evening ends with a heartfelt dance from the East, in which partners gaze deeply into each other's eyes. And the finale of this miracle-play—sweet hugging. We hug in silence, merging with each partner in the One Breath. Long after the dance, we remain in this state of soaring, and the whole world dances with us.

Even after the dances are over, it is still easy to enter into this state of soaring—you just remember the words or the melody of a dance, the eyes of your partners, or simply recall the warmth glowing in your heart.

Throughout our lives each of us has such experiences of soaring—when we learn to walk, to swim, to dance, to paint...

Soaring arouses a person to create, inspiration flows, every contact with this new world produces perfect works of art, whether this manifests as a drawing or a cake recipe, composing a song or building a house, or as a scientific discovery... We often experience soaring in our dreams—while flying, writing poetry, finding lost objects, solving complex scientific equations...

We hope that you, too, can remember such experiences of soaring in your own life.

World View

"Oh, you can't help that," said the Cat. "We're all mad here. I'm mad. You're mad."

"How do you know I'm mad?" said Alice.

"You must be," said the Cat, "or you wouldn't have come here."

Lewis Carroll—*Alice's Adventures in Wonderland*

Reality is imaginary, and the imaginary is real!

Vseslav Solo—*The Fundamentals of Magic*

The world in which we live is a group visualization, which we have been taught to uphold from the day of our birth. In fact, this is really the only thing which one generation passes to another.

Victor Pelevin—*Chapaev and Emptiness*
(a.k.a. *Buddha's Little Finger*)

What we call the physical universe is actually based on agreement. The atom, for example, is simply an agreement among physicists. Now they have come to an agreement on the existence of an even greater number of smaller particles which they cannot even see.

Luke Rhinehart —*Transformation*

It is impossible to comprehend the incomprehensible.

Kozma Prutkov

6

For the past several years, we have attempted to comprehend the laws of the universe, the mechanism of cause and effect, in order to better understand the world we live in. A person—more exactly, the mind—constantly tries to explain what is happening in life: Why some things happen to us, but other things don't work out; why we encounter particular people at a particular time; why some people are loved while others are despised or ignored; why some people are rich while others are poor; some are healthy, but others are ailing.*

We have attempted to discover the answers to these questions in erudite books on esotericism and psychology, and at seminars addressing these themes.

We began our search for truth by practicing Yoga, and therefore fanatically believed in "energy," "chakras," and "Kundalini." We became strict vegetarians, regularly cleansing our organisms of accumulated toxins and, to conserve our sexual energy, we consciously directed it toward spiritual development.

During this time, we pored over many esoteric books and were greatly impressed by the works of Carlos Castaneda and Richard Bach, both of whom still influence us today. In our view, the principal concept in the works of Castaneda is becoming aware of your "description of the world" (we prefer the term "world view")—your perception of the universe which you begin forming at birth (perhaps even at conception), and which is constantly affirmed by an unspoken agreement with the people around you. We call this mutually accepted agreement the *common world view*.

---

* Usually we search for reasons for events which affect us when life's circumstances are unfavorable (i.e., not as we wish them to be). Instead of dwelling on our misfortune, this book proposes a system which uses magical techniques to alter life's circumstances in a favorable direction.

Actually, the common world view is like a religion, whose dogma is rarely discussed; its adherents (most people) are like religious fanatics who unquestioningly believe that it is the one and only truth. Many people fear falling under the influence of some obscure cult, of which there are so many these days (also a component of the common world view). They do not realize that, in fact, they have already belonged to a cult for their entire lives—the religious cult professed by the common world view. Figuratively speaking, each person through the course of a day (and for most even in the night) are constantly intoning prayers like this: "I believe in the regular alternation of day and night, and of the seasons. I believe that people exist and that I am a person, that I have one head, one body, two arms, two legs, and that I belong to a specific gender (not all believe this last part). I believe in the power of money and bow down to its supreme authority. I believe that the earth is round and that it rotates around the sun. I believe in the Law of Gravity. I believe that I will die... In the name of Space, Time, and Matter, Amen!"

"This isn't a matter of faith!" you might exclaim. "It's just speaking the obvious. You can see proof of the laws of nature (i.e., dogmas) anywhere you look; there are no exceptions. And I can prove that I'm right. What if I whacked you over the head with a stick? Then I'd like to hear what you have to say about life being an illusion!"

By all means, we do not want to stick out our necks by challenging the common world view; in fact, we, too, profess it.

"Come on! Even to propose that the common world view is an illusion is some crazy pipe dream!"

It was the writer Richard Bach who profoundly influenced us with ideas about the illusoriness of the world. However, the first strike against the "real world" was inflicted by the works of the great Russian scientist and populist, Nikolay Morozov—*Revelation in Thunder and Storm, The Prophets*, and a series of seven books under the general name of *The Christ*. His works convincingly prove that modern perceptions of ancient history are little more than myth, collections of "historical novels."

Morozov critiques classical views of history, applying data from astronomy, geophysics, paleontology, philology, and many other sciences to support his conclusions. The established historical world view collapses under the onslaught of data he presents from the natural sciences. Not only did Morozov overthrow the classical historical world view, but he also constructed a new way of viewing history out of the wreckage of the old.

A talented man with a rich imagination, he *singlehandedly* constructed this alternate historical world view, while it took the efforts of thousands of scholars to construct the common world view. Morozov's historical world view is stunning! Here are some of the ideas he proposes: the antiquity of the Eastern cultures in India and China is greatly overstated; they appeared in the Middle Ages, later than ancient Rome. Also, Classical Antiquity and the Renaissance were of the same epoch, and, consequently, the "Dark Ages" did not separate them. Ancient Egypt was part of the Roman Empire, and the pharaohs were actually Roman emperors. The Mongol and Tartar invasions of Rus' did not occur, and, in fact, the Mongol and Tartar Khans were Russian princes who had lost in the battle for power taking place in Russia at that time.*

After reading through the works of Morozov, we began to suspect that, in fact, neither the classical historical world view nor Morozov's alternate view truly describes "real history." Most likely, "real history" simply does not exist! Moreover, the common historical view is a direct reflection of the illusion promulgated by the common world view which most people adhere to.

Let's consider how we create our world, more exactly, our common world view.** Suppose that at birth we know nothing, our minds are a "blank slate." We not only don't know that the world is round, but we don't even suspect that the world exists at all. Furthermore, we are completely unaware of physical boundaries, and that we have a body—two arms, two legs, a head, etc. In our mother's womb we perceived the world as a single, complete whole, not divided into separate parts, and we fully identified with this world (the womb).

From immemorial times there has existed a legend in human society, which was never open to question. It states that women only give birth to beings with *human form*, not a baby crocodile or some other kind of wild beast. An expecting mother, naturally, believes in this legend.

While the fetus is developing in the womb, the mother imagines how her newborn baby will look, and if it stirs faintly within her, she "knows" exactly which "part of the body" it is moving. Relatives and friends of the expecting mother are also convinced that she is bearing a small human being. In

---

* Morozov's works on Russian history were never published, but are stored in the archives of the Russian Academy of Sciences. Currently, Morozov's historical world view is being further developed by a group of scientists under the leadership of academician A. T. Fomenko, who is not a professional historian but rather a mathematician. After two decades (grade school, college, graduate school) of buying into the common historical world view, it has been exceedingly difficult to renounce it.

** This is very beautifully and plausibly expressed in a short story by Victor Pelevin "Ivan Kublakhanov."

this way, the people surrounding the child begin to define its features even while in the womb—*they actually help form its physical body*, training it to be an individual being separated off from the rest of the world. The culmination of this process is the moment of birth. The infant, in fact similar to a human being, is inspected by the obstetricians. They touch and probe various parts of its body; they swaddle it. Over time, constant conditioning helps solidify the image of the human form.

"Where are baby's cute little eyes? Now show me mommy's eyes. Here are the doll's eyes... Look: stick, stick, little cucumber—here's the baby!"

While still in the womb, a most important concept begins to take root in the world of the unborn child—*time*. From the moment of conception, two rhythms are constantly present to the fetus—coming from somewhere unknown, it hears the regular beating of a huge metronome (the mother's heart), and its universe continuously expands and contracts with a steady rhythm (the mother's breathing). The child's universe operates according to set routines—during the "night" it rests, during the "day" it is active, etc. Routines continue after birth as well, such as feedings given at strictly determined times.

Next, influenced by its surroundings, the child begins the process of *constructing* various objects in its world. Out of the surrounding chaos, a newborn is taught how to identify people, objects, plants, animals, etc., assigning to each concept concrete, recognizable features. The young child is shown some kind of indistinct blur and hears "Mama, mama, mama...," and gradually the child learns to construct "mama." You might say that, metaphorically, each word names a *slide* collection stored in the memory. For example, behind the word "chair" stand all the images of chairs which the child has seen in its brief existence. In this way, the particular *language* it learns becomes its most important *instrument for creating reality*.

As the child confidently begins to distinguish (material-ize) objects, he learns to link a series of different images into an uninterrupted sequence, filling in absent interrelationships between frames. The internal slides "come to life" and turn into *internal movies*, which have sound, smell, kinetic sensa-tion, etc. He starts understanding entire sentences, represent-ed by the name of the corresponding movie—for example "Mama is cooking oatmeal." At this point, the *law of cause and effect* is introduced:

"Don't touch the stove, or you'll burn your fingers; eat your oatmeal, and I'll give you a treat..."

Figuratively speaking, each person, while growing up, be-comes a storehouse for these internal movies (as Gurdjieff expresses it, turning into a "mechanical person"). The primary movies are created early on, and whenever new information is received from the surrounding world, the child translates it into words, instantly editing its internal movie from available film clips and slides.

The sum total of all these internal movies becomes the person's *world view*.*

Furthermore, each person's world view is unique to him-self or herself, personal. In fact, during social interactions we only give the appearance that we truly understand each other. When we talk to another person, we can only describe our own world view, which may be drastically different from that of the other person.

The world view of a European and a bushman is strikingly different. This is brilliantly portrayed in the film *The Gods Must Be Crazy*. As shown in the film, a bushman perceives a truck as a huge, fast-running wild beast with a head, paws, ears, and tail.

---

* Instead of "world view," it may be more exact to use the phrase "film library," but we will stick to the generally accepted term.

Similarly, the world view of a person who has lost his mind differs just as strikingly from the world view of "normal" people.

How are new objects constructed in the mind? A mental patient in the film *Twelve Monkeys* superbly explains the discovery of microbes in this monologue:

> *You know what "crazy" is? "Crazy" is "majority rules." Take germs, for example. In the 18th century, there was no such thing! Nobody had ever imagined such a thing—no sane person anyway. Along comes this doctor... Samuel Weiss, I think. He tries to convince people, other doctors mostly, that there are these teeny tiny, invisible "bad things" called germs that get into your body and make you... sick! He's trying to get doctors to wash their hands.*
>
> *So cut to the 20th century! Last week, in fact, right before I got dragged into this hellhole. I order a burger in this fast food joint. The waiter drops it on the floor. He picks it up, wipes it off, hands it to me... like it was all okay. "What about the germs?" I say. He goes: "I don't believe in germs. Germs are just a plot they made up so they can sell you disinfectants and soap!"*
>
> *Now, he's crazy, right? Hey, you believe in germs, don't you? There's only "majority rules." There is no right, no wrong... Only what everyone thinks is true.*

We would add that the further materialization of microbes followed as would be expected—scientists saw them in microscopes, discovered new types, classified them, etc.

In a similar way, the AIDS virus was created not long ago. The process is described in detail by James P. Hogan in the chapter "AIDS Heresy and the New Bishops" of his book *Rockets, Redheads and Revolution.**

Citing the research of Peter Duesberg, professor of molecular and cellular biology at the University of California, Berkeley, Hogan presents a convincing argument that AIDS in reality does not exist, that the entire epidemic has been created out of thin air for profit. We will briefly cite here a few of his conclusions.

At the end of the 1980's, Duesberg published an article stating that AIDS could not possibly have arisen from HIV—in fact, from any kind of virus at all. Duesberg performed a detailed analysis of the correspondence between AIDS and four criteria for infectious diseases known as Koch's Postulates. He ascertained that, regarding the theory that HIV causes AIDS, not one of these criteria were fulfilled—i.e., AIDS is not infectious!

He believes that the reason for inventing AIDS is obvious.

While searching for a cure for polio in the beginning of the 1960's, American medical research institutions graduated a large number of virologists. When this task was finally completed, all the human and institutional resources which had been required for the polio epidemic began seeking another crusade to embark on—to discover a cure for the "new deadly virus" and to produce a vaccine to combat it. Federal expenditures grew annually to billions of dollars. Never before had the scientific-medical establishment and the bureaucrats managing it received such a generous largesse.

Serving the victims of AIDS was funded at the public expense, which meant lucrative consultation fees, costly testing, and medical procedures involving the most expensive drugs. Researchers, who otherwise would have spent their

---

* Hogan, James P. *Rockets, Redheads and Revolution*. Riverdale NY: Baen Books, 1999.

lives peering into microscopes and washing out Petri dishes, became millionaires by founding companies to manufacture HIV testing equipment and materials, and to charge patients money for performing the tests.

For his attacks against this "Golden Calf," Duesberg—a pioneer in researching retroviruses, recipient of a seven-year Outstanding Investigator Grant from the National Institutes of Health, and candidate for the Nobel Prize for his work in discovering oncogenes—was greeted by howls of abuse and scorn, his theories discredited, and his research grants sharply reduced.

You may ask: "Even if we do grant that AIDS was, indeed, invented, people are still dying from it."

Duesberg maintains that they are dying not from AIDS but rather from a range of diseases connected with immunodeficiency: pneumonia, tuberculosis, various infections, etc. However, our feeling is that they are, in fact, dying from the common world view, which considers AIDS to be an incurable disease. All world views reside in the mind, and when a person focuses on a particular issue, his imagination bestows it with life, and the accepted model becomes active.

Hogan has painted quite an impressive picture of the world! No wonder physicians have so strenuously sought out ever new and more terrible diseases, and the mass media continues to diligently report their discoveries. Fortunately, they have not yet been able to achieve global acceptance for a new replacement for AIDS.

The principal method by which new objects are introduced into the common world view is simple. A person with a rich imagination creates a movie which did not previously exist. As long as the movie lives only in the consciousness of a single "madman," it is dangerous to proclaim the new discovery to the world; they will just send him to the nuthouse. In order for a newly invented phenomenon to be accepted as real, you have to convince everyone around you that it does indeed exist. Actually, you only have to convince a small group of authoritative people—scientists, politicians, the mass media—and it is as good as done. The delusion becomes public property, a component of the mass hallucination. This model has been persuasively described in the fantasy novel by Colin Wilson *The Mind Parasites*.

The authority to construct new formations in the modern, civilized world is entrusted mainly to scientists (the high priests of the religion which professes the common world view). Consider the experience of Dmitry Ivanovich Mendeleev, who in a dream saw a rectangular table with cells containing the known chemical elements. Many of the cells, however, were still empty, but these were to be later filled in by as yet undiscovered elements, whose qualities were derived from their position in the table. No sooner had the world finished applauding his genius than these new elements began to be discovered, popping up like mushrooms after a spring shower. But what if Mendeleev had dreamed up a table in the shape of a doughnut? Or if he had attempted to construct his classification in three dimensions?

We can only imagine how many great discoveries and inventions are buried in the back rooms of psycho wards!

Not long ago, we were on our way to a distant city to present a workshop. The radio in the train compartment was turned on, and the announcer was saying:

"Physicists from Dubna Research Center near Moscow have succeeded in synthesizing a new 114th element on the Periodic Table of Mendeleev. They report that it remained in existence for a full 30(!) seconds. This is a great discovery, inasmuch as previous newly discovered elements have lasted for only microseconds(!!)."

This requires no commentary.

"Aha!" an astute reader might exclaim. "From what you say, all our troubles come out of the common world view! In that case, we may as well just gather up all the books of the world and burn them! To think that they even invented AIDS!"

If no one shares your world view, and it is fundamentally different from the common view, then you will be proclaimed insane, and they will isolate you from all the other lunatics who are deluded by the common world view. Therefore, you can reject the common world view, yet you must still remember its basic tenets.

If you eliminate the common world view, then you will have to invent a new collective illusion. This is not an easy task, since it is something which can only be achieved by civilization as a whole.

Thought is Material

Once while passing through a city,
I saw no people anywhere.
On every building, every house,
Were only mirrors everywhere.

If I smiled cheerfully,
The city smiled back at me;
And if I greeted anyone,
That person also greeted me.

At times the city seemed alive,
With people all around me.
Now I know I'm all alone,
And only mirrors surround me.

Andrey Makarevich—The Crystal City

"What *is* the matter?" she said, as soon as there was a chance of making herself heard. "Have you pricked your finger?"

"I haven't pricked it *yet*," the Queen said, "but I soon shall—oh, oh, oh!"

"When do you expect to do it?" Alice asked, feeling very much inclined to laugh.

"When I fasten my shawl again," the poor Queen groaned out. "The brooch will come undone directly. Oh!

Oh!" As she said the words the brooch flew open, and the Queen clutched wildly at it, and tried to clasp it again. "Take care!" cried Alice. "You're holding it all crooked!" And she caught at the brooch; but it was too late: the pin had slipped, and the Queen had pricked her finger.

Lewis Carroll—*Alice through the Looking Glass*

This book utilizes popular theory on thought materialization. In our world view, this means that internal movies can be materialized. To demonstrate this theory, we will trace the development of two scenarios.*

I was sitting at the computer, typing. The radio was on, and the broadcaster announced that David Copperfield had just publicly confessed.**

I thought: "I've always known that he's an illusionist, pretending to do real magic. I wonder how much they paid him for his confession? People are so greedy these days."

Suddenly, I heard a scuffle and loud cussing outside my window.

"And uncultured, too! Why can't they just smash in each other's faces without all the cussing? Times are hard, and people are pissed off! Prices have skyrocketed. If this goes on, I won't have enough money to even feed my family."

---

* The concept of thought materialization is frequently encountered in psychotherapy—particularly, in neuro-linguistic programming. In psychology, it is believed that thoughts influence a person's emotions and feelings. We would go further to say that "external reality" itself is created by one's thoughts and emotions.

** We made this up. So much as we know, Copperfield has never confessed.

At that point, I heard a key slip into the keyhole.

"Oh, no! My wife! And I forgot to go to the store. I'm in trouble now!"

My wife gave me quite a dressing down, shouting about how she was exhausted from work, and not only had I forgotten to go to the store, but I hadn't fed the kid either.

"Things aren't right here!" I thought. "How come the man is supposed to go shopping, cook, wash the dishes, clean up, and do the laundry?"

These sullen thoughts swirled around my mind that night, keeping me awake until the early morning. I woke up with a horrendous headache...

These events could have unfolded in a different scenario. Hearing the broadcast about Copperfield, I could have responded by thinking:

"In a way, everyone's an illusionist. And if he managed all that time to pull the wool over people's eyes (like the Great Houdini), and no one could see through his tricks, then all power to him. Certainly many people, if even for a few moments, truly believed that he was flying. Sing praise to the great illusionists!"

I heard this song on the radio:

> All guile, deceit has flown away,
> No sham left to be seen,
> Illusion's face is blown away
> And smashed to smithereens.
>
> But still I wish in my heart an' all
> To save from such extremes
> At least a tiny particle
> Of all my rosy dreams.

Over rosy fragments tumbling,
I dance barefoot all around
I'm not in the least bit grumbling
That my hope's turned upside down.*

"Good song! I wish someone from our group would sing such a song about magicians."

Then, by the way my wife slipped the key into the keyhole, I knew immediately that she was in a great mood. And so it was—my better half was trying on the dress she'd purchased and asked me how it looked on her.

"Yes, my wife's amazing—it doesn't take much to put her in a good mood."

She cooked us a delicious dinner, and we shared a wonderful evening together. The next morning a brilliant idea came to me...

We have looked at two different scenarios in which thoughts influenced the progression of events. In the first, while listening to the broadcast about Copperfield, I immediately started playing my internal movie about bourgeois greed, which was projected into the scuffle and loud cussing; and this, in its turn, aroused feelings about future difficulties awaiting me...

These two scenarios, which here were greatly simplified, demonstrate how events could possibly unfold—either "negatively" or "positively." Usually switching between scenarios occurs chaotically, and so life's successes are "mixed," as expressed in the popular song: "After joy will come sorrow— and who knows what tomorrow."

* This song was translated by John Woodsworth. [trans]

This example shows that what's important isn't the message we receive from the outer world, but rather our *response* to it. The message is neither "good" nor "bad"— I am the one who evaluates it, who attaches to it a particular emotional coloring.

Inasmuch as thought is material, it is evident that each moment of my life *I create my own world*. Everything around me is an extension of myself, the materialization of my personal world view.

Mindfulness

I do not weep, I do not cry.
Just ask me, friend, I will not lie.
All life's a game, and who's to blame?
I love this life, I'm glad I came!
Song of Ostap Bender—The Twelve Chairs
(as sung by Andrey Mironov)

You walk into the theater: there's going to be battles and excitement, winners and losers, romance, disaster; you know that's all going to be there.

We buy tickets to these films, paying admission by agreeing to believe in the reality of space and the reality of time... Neither one is true, but anyone who doesn't want to pay that price cannot appear on this planet, or in any space-time system at all.
Richard Bach—Illusions

You like to play when you know you can't lose, don't you?... An all-knowing expression of perfect Life has to reject all-knowingness and claim five senses only...

Do you think you're invited to play with the rest of us when you don't follow our rules? Who do you think is going to play with you?
Richard Bach—Running from Safety

We offer here yet another possible world view. Let's pretend that *we really are all immortal, all-powerful beings—magicians.*

This raises the question: What do immortal beings do? How could they possibly fill all that time? The answer is— they amuse themselves... And how do they do that? With *games*, of course!

Once Papa* asked his nine-year-old son Nikita a question: "What do you think? Why are we here in this world?"

The computer gamer's answer was lightening quick: "To while away time."

To an immortal being, all that's left to do is to pleasantly pass the time, to play. A favorite game might be to totally forget your immortality and to play the mortality game of life and death. Truly, this is a most amazing game—full of surprise, success, and disappointment, pleasure and suffering, and, of course, with an unpredictable ending. "Game over!" and then what?

Imagine that we really are immortal magicians, who, having created this world, now just want to amuse ourselves, to play this mortality game within the confines of the common world view. In order to make the game more interesting, we forget about our magical abilities and *begin identifying with the players.*

What do you think? Why do some women love soap operas so passionately? Or read romance novels? Or cry all the way through a Bollywood movie? Why do men bellow, shout, and whistle at a soccer game? And when someone makes a shot for the goal, they all involuntarily kick out with their leg. The answer is obvious—women identify with heroines; they live through them. But men identify with the players.

---

* Beard and Papa are the authors' nicknames. [trans]

And how is the soap opera discussed? "Well, *I* would never have allowed Louis Albert even onto my doorstep!"

Here is another example. A child is playing on the computer for several hours, then suddenly bursts into tears: "I've been playing this game for so long and finally reached the seventh level! And then *I got killed*!"

But with grown-ups, when they get virtually "killed" or their favorite team allows (or scores) a goal, they'll up and die of a heart attack, collapsing right down onto the keyboard, or in front of the television.

We offer up the metaphor elucidated by Sergey Lukianenko in his fantasy novel *The Maze of Reflections*. The novel's hero writes an exceptional program, which allows anyone with a computer to enter a virtual world. The images on the screen become the player's actual experience. Gradually, he becomes deeply submerged into the virtual Depths—as a soldier, for example, he learns that cartridge-cases are hot, and that the recoil from a grenade launcher can knock you off your feet. He soon forgets that everything around him is fantasy, an illusion, and that he is sitting at the keyboard. The only way for him to quit the game and come out of his stupor is to get through to the very end, or to die a lonely death in that virtual reality.

Sometimes, though, you encounter gamers (only a few), so-called divers, who do not ever lose their connection with reality; at any moment they can emerge fully from the Depths of the playing space—maybe to knock down a cold drink before a wild virtual adventure, or to launch some program which allows them to overcome more easily all the horrible dangers lying in wait for them in the Depths.

If I become one of these divers—that is, if I don't identify with the picture shown on the screen (in our model, with someone who plays according to the rules of the common world view), but rather with the person sitting at the keyboard (the magician)—then, at just the right moment, I can quit the game (change the world around me).

What does mindfulness consist of? Remembering that *"I am a magician, and I, too, live in this illusory world, this projection of the common world view,"* and that *"I can change this world by connecting into the world of magic."* I do not believe that what happens in my life is inevitable; instead I respond to events by consciously choosing the most desirable outcome.

If necessary, I set my intention to creatively alter the situation. To manifest a chosen outcome, I enter into a magical state (*I can do anything!*)—eyes ablaze, heart sensuously warm, feeling like I'm on the verge of taking off into space…

This poem was written by a magician, who, in an attempt to increase her income, was hunting crocodiles while sitting naked on the edge of her bathtub, gently dipping her butt as bait into the water.

> Magic! Such a wondrous dream!
> Joyously it makes us free.
> May those who stipulate the rules
> Be bound themselves by their decree.
>
> From now on I'll strive to keep
> Only things which make me smile.
> Happily I'm dipping down
> My butt to lure a crocodile.

Since all world views are illusions, the magician laughs at the "rules of the game" and the "laws of the universe"—and at his own world view, too. He acts in *comedy theater* as opposed to the dramatic theater so adored by the rest of humanity. All the world is a theater of the absurd, pure hocus-pocus, distraction and mystification; why would you take any of it seriously? Instead, playful rituals like the crocodile hunt above are performed with joy, and miracles begin to happen...

This approach differs fundamentally from traditional conceptions, even from the theory of karma which is so fashionable these days. The beautiful karmic theater impresses by its drama. The idea of karma implies a heavy weight of sins and transgressions from the past. The only way to extirpate them is through repentance, penitence, and suffering, atoning for past mistakes over the course of a lifetime (or many lifetimes). Having ourselves once believed in the concept of karma, the question always rankled us: How can I possibly keep living with this impossibly heavy burden?! And what's more, it is we ourselves who have loaded this weight onto our own shoulders, having bought into the idea of karma, which, like any other world view, is really just another mass hallucination.

To be totally free while playing in the theater of cause and effect is extremely difficult—so much has already been absorbed into the personality. However, if you relate to karma in a light and easygoing way, with humor, then expiation of karma happens rather quickly and without suffering. You can absolve your karma over the course of your entire life (or over many lifetimes), or you can free yourself in a matter of months, days, hours, even minutes. Sometimes with a single, joyful wink, or skipping around playfully—and a thousand years of karma simply disappears without a trace.

Giving Thanks

We don't take bribes, but we do accept tips.

Russian proverb

We have nothing to be afraid of except our fear.

Aphorism of a friend

There is no such thing as a problem without a gift for you in its hands. You seek problems because you need their gifts.

Richard Bach—*Illusions*

Once upon a time in a land far away, there lived a King and Queen. They had a daughter, Frosia, who was indescribably beautiful. The King had long considered how best to choose a worthy husband for the princess, when one night he had a dream, in which he saw his daughter imprisoned in a dark cave on a distant, unknown island named Buyan. This dream proved to be prophetic for soon thereafter the princess disappeared. Messengers were sent throughout the kingdom and ambassadors went overseas to proclaim the imperial decree: "Whoever finds the royal princess shall win her hand in marriage together with half the kingdom."

Princes and mighty warriors, merchants and common people responded to the call. The path to the island Buyan led through many dangerous trials and tribulations, requiring great deeds of strength, persistence, and courage. The trait most needed, however, was an unshakable belief in oneself. All these qualities were best shown by a peasant's son, Feodor.

While searching for the princess, Feodor became lost in a dense forest. Eventually, he came upon a faint trail which led him to a huge, moss-covered boulder. Through the moss and mold, Feodor could barely make out the inscription: "Go left and lose your head; go straight and find Koshchey;* go right and vanish into cyberspace!" Feodor sat down in deep thought. He didn't notice when an old woman, Dundusa, appeared before him out of nowhere.

"Why are you so sad, my friend? Why do you hang your head?"

"Don't disturb my thoughts, old woman. I'm miserable enough without you."

"You are not polite to your elders, Feodor."

"Get out of here, you old hag!"

"Take heed, Feodor, or you will regret this," the old woman warned, and she gradually melted into thin air.

It was late. Feodor was exhausted and fell into a heavy sleep. In his dream, Feodor was paddling down a turbulent river, the Kryamzha. Passing under a bridge, he caught a quick snatch of conversation: "It's such a terrible year for cranberries in the Vargun Bogs!"

The thought passed through his mind: "What do the Vargun Bogs have to do with me?"

Feodor felt hungry. He dragged his boat up a steep bank, lit a small fire, and cooked up a savory fish soup. Before eating, Feodor gulped down a slug of homebrew from his flask.

---

* In Russian folklore, Koshchey is an evil sorcerer of terrifying appearance, a shape-shifter, who often takes the form of a whirlwind. He is a nature spirit representing the destructive powers of nature. According to some sources, Koshchey might originally have been a kind wizard, whose image was gradually corrupted over time. [trans]

Suddenly, a sharp whistle startled him. Feodor peered across the river and gasped in astonishment. Dundusa was standing there, whistling at him and desperately waving her arms.

"What do you want, old woman?"

"Row me across the river, my dear."

"There's no time. I'm searching for my princess."

"Can't we just have a quick smoke together?"

"I don't smoke, old woman. I lead a healthy life."

Feodor continued on in his boat. For some time he pondered: "Why didn't I help that old woman? She was all alone there in the dark forest. Oh, to hell with her! She can take care of herself."

That night, while Feodor was sleeping soundly, someone stole his sword which bore the inscription: "For victory over the dragon Gorynych."

"There are thieves everywhere here! These borderlands are going to the dogs," he said indignantly. "Next time I'll camp further away from the village." But this did not comfort him at all.

The next day, still aggravated, Feodor became careless and did not notice a snag hidden amongst the weeds. At full speed, his boat crashed into the snag and flipped over. With difficulty he at last managed to reach the shore. So now all he had left was an old boat with a hole in it. Everything else had been swept away by the swift current. Feodor's teeth chattered violently; he just couldn't warm himself. His matches were all wet, and lighters were not yet invented. He began to feel feverish; his whole body was shaking. "When it rains, it pours!" Feodor managed to think as he was losing consciousness. "But there's nothing to be done. Life's tough for everyone these days."

When Feodor came to, the first thing he saw was Dundusa's familiar, wrinkled face.

"So, my dear friend, what mischief have you been up to?" she asked. "Now listen carefully to what I tell you:

"Once my nephew, the Mullah Nasrudin, couldn't make his donkey budge for anything, stopping him short on his journey to Mecca. Exhausted, he lay down to rest under a fig tree growing at the edge of a watermelon patch. Nasrudin looked at the watermelons, then at the fig tree and thought: 'Everything in this world is backwards. Those small vines bear huge melons, while this tall tree has only tiny figs.'

"The Mullah slipped into deep meditation, when suddenly a fig fell down from the tree, striking him on the head. This was so unexpected that he jumped up and, looking upwards, he saw a large monkey about to throw a whole handful of figs at him. The Mullah began thanking the monkey profusely.

"*'Thank you, monkey, for showing me that, if my every wish came true, then I wouldn't be able to thank you at all, since I would be buried beneath a whole pile of watermelons. How can I thank you enough?'*

"The monkey listened to this inspired discourse, still holding its handful of figs. Then the greatest magician of all time fished his prayer beads out of the folds of his robe and threw them up to the monkey. The monkey nimbly caught the beads and immediately hung them around its neck. The figs fell out of its hand, which caught the attention of the donkey, which ran over and started eating them. 'Eureka!' the Mullah exclaimed in a flash of realization.

"That's when he realized how to manage a stubborn donkey, and he immediately put his idea into practice. His donkey trotted happily after a bundle of hay hung on a stick in front of its nose, and the stick was attached to the body of the donkey."

Finishing her story, Dundusa began slowly evaporating into a rainbow cloud, which at last dissipated completely.

Feodor woke up and saw the same moss-covered boulder. He had hardly come back to his senses, when he heard a wild shout and crashing of branches. A furry ball rolled onto the footpath directly in front of him, scattering tufts of fur everywhere. Reaching Feodor, the ball split in half, and two demons stood before him. Cutting short their fight, they exclaimed gleefully: "Now we'll gobble you up, human!"

Feodor's hand, as usual, reached for his sword, but, seeing his movement, the demons burst into a wild frenzy of laughter. The older one took a toy cannon out of his pocket, which, in the twinkle of an eye, grew to full size.

"You still want to mess with us, little Feodor? You may have your humanity, but we have sorcery!" sneered the younger devil.

Feodor knew that he could not escape by running. He remembered his dream, and he could still hear Dundusa's voice uttering her parting words: *Do not retreat and do not fight back, be nothing.* It dawned on Feodor that he should help the demons settle their conflict.

"Cease, cursed demons! Why are you fighting?"

"Our father died and we inherited a sack of gold, but we can't agree on how to divide it."

"That's not a problem. I can help you."

"If you cheat us, we'll eat you, but if you help us, we'll reward you well."

Feodor slyly winked at the older demon and suggested that he divide up the gold as evenly as possible. The older demon quickly split the gold into two piles. Then Feodor told the younger one to choose which pile he wanted. Both demons were happy with this solution.

"You are truly Solomon the Wise," rejoiced the demons, and they disappeared into the ground. At the very spot where they had vanished, a brand-new flying carpet appeared, still smelling of fresh dye. As Feodor took off flying up into the air, he noticed an inscription on the edge of the carpet: *There is always a way out!*

To understand how we deal with life's problems, we offer the following typical situation. Imagine that I'm walking down a dark street and notice the threatening figure of a street thug standing in my path. Fear rises inside me. In my imagination the pertinent movie automatically starts up, showing the thug coming up to me: "Gimme your wallet or I'll kill you!" I am already considering possible reactions—give him my money, knock him to the ground, turn and run. There are problems with each of these possible scenarios: I would hate to give up my hard-earned cash; I myself could end up being the one on the ground; and the thug (let's call him Ivan) might be a championship runner. What should I do? Or in the words of Hamlet: "To be, or not to be: that is the question: Whether 'tis nobler in the mind to suffer the slings and arrows of outrageous fortune [give him my money]. Or to take arms against a sea of troubles [carry mace]…"

For a magician, these questions make no sense whatsoever. Ivan indicates to the magician that it is time to get to work, to prove to himself that he is a magician.

Remember that at this point nothing has yet happened; the thug is still far away from me. Perhaps he hasn't even noticed me.

When a magician encounters a thug in a dark alleyway, he might say something like this (not necessarily out loud!):

"Thank you, Vanya, *for warning me that what I am imagining could actually happen to me: you could beat me up and take all my money. Then I might become like you, or end up begging for money at bus stops, since my wife would never let me come home without any money."*

---

* *Vanya, Vanechka* (both stressed on the first syllabus)—endearing forms of the masculine name *Ivan*. [trans]

By speaking the thanksgiving monologue, we add a soundtrack to the "negative" internal movie which is showing in our mind. We can keep adding to it even to the point of absurdity, making it completely ridiculous. It is a well-known fact that expressing one's fear weakens it—the devil (fear) is not so terrible as he is painted (by people in their minds). The reason for this is that we pull fear out of the "subconscious" into the "conscious" mind, thus removing any "suppression."

The thanksgiving monologue is only the first part of the act of thanksgiving, but its recitation can instantly relieve the situation—for instance, someone might call out to the thug, distracting him, or a police car may pass by, or friends could emerge out of the next doorway; I might even exchange a few words with the thug and discover that we went to the same kindergarten, and so on.

It is important to note that, if fear did not rise in me when I first saw the thug, then I would not have to thank him.

I can "strengthen" the thanksgiving by sending Ivan *an imaginary gift*.

Imagine that someone picked out a gift for you, which was not only exactly what you wanted but was wrapped up in beautiful wrapping paper. We enjoy attractive packaging—a slender woman passing by, a shiny new Cadillac, a beautifully decorated cake, a well-dressed gentleman. There is a Russian proverb: "People meet your clothes, but accompany your mind."

While creating this imaginary picture, boundless scope for creativity opens up to the magician. He is not limited by the size of his canvas, range of colors, or rules prescribing his design. The artist prefers unusual images for these pictures, although there are also magicians who keep to a strict "classical" style. If we paint a tree, we might replace its fruit with doughnuts or soap bubbles, and the treetops could consist of colorful umbrellas. Russian fairytales are abundant in such images—Baba Yaga's hut on chicken legs, rivers of milk with jelly banks, the Frog Princess. In a more realistic style, we might paint the tree with a branchy top, a powerful root system, and thick, succulent leaves.

Now we can complete the act of thanksgiving for Ivan the thug:

"Thank you, Vanya, for warning me that what I am imagining could actually happen to me: you could beat me up and take all my money. Then I might become like you, or end up begging for money at bus stops, since my wife would never let me come home without any money. For warning me of this, I thank you and offer you a crane wearing rubber boots, which is painting a fence green with a vacuum cleaner."

During thanksgiving the gift may be transformed, and not only once. Beginning with a crane with a vacuum cleaner, we could leap to a monkey with a contrabass, which in turn could be transformed into a cave on the seashore, and so on. *Remember, the picture doesn't change by itself; it is you who draws and colors it in.*

You can close your eyes to help make your picture more vivid. If you are having difficulty creating the picture, just begin with any object which catches your eye. Suppose you see a button which you turn into a flying saucer, then a lake, a hockey puck, etc. After the initial image has been constructed, it is easy to adorn it with details.

In order to activate the imagination, we recommend that you bring sound to the process of drawing. Suppose that I am sitting in the kitchen, watching a running faucet. I say aloud: "I am drawing a waterfall in the mountains which hurls Feodor along in a barrel. He sits in it like Baba Yaga steering with a paddle, which he rented from a plaster statue at the Pioneer Camp 'Young Cavalryman.' On the bank below him, a Red Army soldier, Sukhov, greets him with traditional bread and salt. Sukhov is accompanied by freed women from the East, who are singing 'Like a snowflake, I melt in your arms…'"

We generally prefer to paint humorous pictures which are way over-the-top. When painting the crane, for instance, we place it in unusual circumstances. Every picture should have its own zest. A humorous frame of mind helps us create pictures easily, even playfully. Besides the visual channel, you can switch on the sound channel, and the sensory channel as well. As regards the crane, this could be the roar and vibration of the vacuum cleaner, the smell of paint, etc.

Let's look even deeper into the thanksgiving monologue. First, I thank the obstacle for warning me that my fear could be materialized. Remember, when the thug appeared, I immediately began playing in my imagination the horror movie called "How I Was Robbed" or "The Time I Got Beat Up." During the thanksgiving monologue, I add appropriate sound to the movie—more precisely, to its script—right up to its tragic finale. It is this tragic ending which really terrifies me.

Since magicians are such joyful people, the final scene in the thanksgiving monologue may even border on the grotesque. They intentionally lay it on so thick that it is impossible to stay serious, especially considering the reason for making this movie.

Consider how the obstacle strengthened in Feodor's dream as he paddled further down the Kryamzha River: the snatch of conversation heard about a bad cranberry harvest in a remote bog, his meal disrupted by Dundusa's whistle, the theft of his sword, crashing his boat, his illness. This is the thanksgiving monologue which Feodor should have recited immediately as he passed beneath the bridge:

"I thank you all for warning me that my journey is in peril. A poor harvest of potatoes and other crops may result in widespread

hunger. Gangs of bandits might appear in the forest, who will begin robbing tourists, and I could be stripped naked and hung by my feet from a tall pine tree..."

As a result of this thanksgiving, Feodor's dream would change, and this would influence daytime events. Feodor might receive a sign about what to do. It could be from a passing crow showing him the way he must travel, or the piercing shriek of an owl, or a leaf falling from a tree. But instead our hero had to sort things out with the demons.

If an act of thanksgiving is done with inspiration, in a single breath, you will not need to wait for results. Because of your creative state of mind, fear of the thug just disappears. However, if under the inertia of thinking fear returns, it is sufficient to remember the gift, or to make up a new one. If you get tired of the same, unchanging image of your gift, then you can further embellish the picture, enriching it with new detail—for instance, the crane might write a slogan on the green fence, which states: "Stand firm, little Mary!"

It is not by accident that we named the thug "Ivan." For convenience magicians have agreed to call all obstacles and problems by the generalized name—*Vanya*, or *dear Vanya*. This is especially handy when working with pain, fear, discomfort, and lack of self-confidence, when there is no specific object obstructing you (the thug in our example). However, a woman magician we know could not bear such discrimination against women and decided to name the obstacle Manya.*

By means of thanksgiving, the obstacle is transformed into success. The subject of such transfiguration is constantly encountered in Russian fairytales—Ivan the Fool, having passed through a thousand difficult trials, becomes Ivan the Prince.

---

* *Manya*—an endearing form of the feminine name *Maria*. [trans]

Results of Magical Acts

Of course, no one would say that Neznaika was hopelessly lazy. Once he learned to read properly, he would spend entire days with his books. He did not read books which were important, but rather books which were interesting, mainly fairytales... Neznaika often said that, if he had a magic wand, he could learn everything without trying; in fact, he would not need to learn anything at all, just wave his magic wand.

Nikolay Nosov —*Neznaika in Sun City*

When we plan neither for a definite result nor for sufficient time to attain it (not engaging the common world view), then the outcome often exceeds our wildest expectations.

Magicians have adopted a humorous unit of measurement—the "magical" number 27. To the question "When can I expect a positive outcome?" magicians answer: "In 27." They never specify what unit the reply is given in.

When I am soaring, all my intentions are realized. If an obstacle rises up to hinder me, I just remember that I am a magician and take creative action (e.g., express thankfulness). The world responds to my creativity, revealing the *best outcome for all participants* in this universal theater called life. I return to my state of soaring, and the situation resolves itself, often in a wholly unexpected way.

This is what happened to the magician Anna, who could not get along with a woman who worked under her. Finally, Anna decided to send her thanks—literally the next day, her subordinate found a better paying job and quit. They were both winners in this outcome.

A magician *does not plan the outcome, does not expect any particular result, and is prepared for anything—but hopes for the best.* This is the basic difference between the joyful magic presented in this book and wizardry, sorcery, and other systems which work for a particular result by imposing the will of the individual onto the outside world. You might say that the magician *invites* all the world to dance. Magicians are like the Russian fairytale character Emelia, who spends his day lounging around on the stove, while overseeing all the processes of the universe.

Techniques for Renaming

"I come from under the hill, and under the hills and over the hills my paths led. And through the air. I am he that walks unseen."—"So I can well believe," said Smaug, "but that is hardly your usual name."—"I am the clue-finder, the web-cutter, the stinging fly. I was chosen for the lucky number."—"Lovely titles!" sneered the dragon. "But lucky numbers don't always come off."—"I am he that buries his friends alive and drowns them and draws them alive again from the water. I came from the end of a bag, but no bag went over me."—"These don't sound so creditable," scoffed Smaug."—"I am the friend of bears and the guest of eagles. I am Ringwinner and Luckwearer; and I am Barrel-rider," went on Bilbo beginning to be pleased with his riddling.

J.R.R. Tolkien—*The Hobbit*

"It is stupid for you to scorn the mysteries of the world simply because you know the doing of scorn," he said with a serious facc.

I assured him that I was not scorning anything or any one, but that I was more nervous and incompetent than he thought.

"I've always been that way," I said. "And yet I want to change, but I don't know how. I am so inadequate."

"I already know that you think you are rotten," he said. "That's your *doing*. Now in order to affect that *doing* I am going to recommend that you learn another *doing*. From now on, and for a period of eight days, I want you to lie to yourself. Instead of telling yourself the truth, that you are ugly and rotten and inadequate, you will tell yourself that you are the complete opposite, knowing that you are lying and that you are absolutely beyond hope."

"But what would be the point of lying like that, don Juan?"

"It may hook you to another doing and then you may realize that both doings are lies, unreal, and that to hinge yourself to either one is a waste of time, because the only thing that is real is the being in you that is going to die. To arrive at that being is the not-doing of the self."

Carlos Castaneda—*Journey to Ixtlan*

The following legend is from a book by Deepak Chopra, *The Way of the Wizard*. One day Merlin pointed to King Arthur and offered a pouch of gold dust to anyone who could say who he truly was. There were various answers: the son of Uther Pendragon, the English Monarch, the flower of Albion, and so forth. In the end, Merlin cast the gold dust out the window, explaining that only the wind had given the correct answer—for the wind cannot speak.

Like King Arthur, each one of us has a number of roles and *masks* which we use while acting in the theater of life. In fact, the personality is this collection of masks. You can give a specific name to a particular mask, describing it in words, which is what King Arthur's courtiers did.

Since thought is material, we would state further that the environment around us corresponds to the particular mask which we wear. *When we change the mask, the circumstances around us likewise change*, as happened to the ugly duckling. As a chick it was relentlessly abused by the other birds, but when it finally matured into a beautiful swan, all birds sang its praises.

There is a well-known Zen Buddhist parable: Once a monk was being chased by a tiger. Running to escape, he reached the edge of a cliff. He climbed down a vine which hung over the edge only to see another tiger waiting at the bottom. At that point a mouse started nibbling at the vine. Caught in this predicament, the monk noticed a ripe strawberry growing off the face of the cliff. He stretched out his arm and tasted it. It was the most delicious berry he'd ever eaten! In the end the monk was saved; otherwise, he could never have told his story.

This brings us to the idea of *renaming* (switching the mask). The *diagnostic name* (old mask) of the monk sounds like this: "I am the one who is hanging by a vine being gnawed by a mouse, while tigers above and below lie in wait for me." But his new name is: *"I am the one who is eating a wild strawberry."*

Suppose an obstacle appears before me. I simply remember that I'm a magician and select a new mask. Consequently, my environment signals: "All OK!" And the obstacle disappears.

We need specific names to achieve our practical goals—*a formula for soaring (i.e., magical names)*. Here are some examples of these magical names: *"I am the one who serves my mother tea and raspberry preserves." "I am the one who elegantly pulls my pants up over my round belly." "I am Frekenbok who calls from the shower."*

In any magical act, the principal element is creativity—the free play of the imagination—so there is no requirement even to adhere to the formula "I am the one who...," or to think up any particular name. For example, participants at our seminars have achieved effective results using very unusual names like *"I am ordinary Soviet bamboo," "a Suck Hundred Mercedes," "a coat-hanger with yellow ears," "I am a lactating elephant with an evergreen trunk," "a sailor's splendid ass plying the great beer sea,"* or *"a real Indian is all right by me."*

Instead of renaming myself, I can instead rename the obstacle; after all, I am the one who created that obstacle (as well as everything else in my world view). For example, I often conflict with my mother-in-law. Her diagnostic name is: "I am the one who always makes a scene," but her new name has become: *"I am the one who tenderly pets the kitten."* In creating these names, it must be emphasized that my mother-in-law is in fact *me*. Instead of renaming my mother-in-law, I can rename my own being. *"I am the one who builds a shelf for my mother-in-law."* In the end, it does not really matter who is renamed; most important is to act creatively, and with good humor.

You may ask: "How long do I have to repeat a new name?" The amount of time is not determined by objective law—one person may require 27 seconds to resolve a complex problem, another 27 years, and a third 27 lifetimes. If I can laugh while watching myself "fettered" by some dramatic situation, then I will be freed fairly quickly.

To develop mindfulness, it is good to affirm my new name each time I notice myself falling back to my former name. If it is a long-standing name, then too many impressions are connected with it. For example, I have lived with my wife for ten years, and I have loved her for all these years. Suppose she suddenly leaves me for Ivan Ivanovich. Many different signals remain to remind me of her—a melody we would dance to, the park where we walked together, the smell of her perfume, her clothes, voice, our mutual friends... Instead of the old diagnostic name: "I am the one whose wife ran out on him," I must keep returning to my new name, and the situation manages in some way to resolve itself— my wife may come back, or I will meet the woman of my dreams, or perhaps women will cease to interest me...

Manifesting creativity, magicians not only repeat the new name, but also play it out in life. They dress up in silly costumes, utilizing attributes appropriate to the image they want to cultivate; they often compose verse, songs, or just some silly ditty. We will cover this in greater detail in the second part of this book, *Magical Stories*.

In this next section we will present specific renaming techniques.

Renaming by Searching for the Root

Look to the root!

Kozma Prutkov

Feodor rode his magic carpet for a long time, or was it a short time? He was intoxicated by his good fortune and did not notice a small speck which appeared in the clear, blue sky. Soon the speck grew into a small cloud. Finally seeing it, Feodor felt somewhat vexed, but at that point his attention was distracted by the witch Baba Yaga, laughing hysterically, as she zoomed past in her jet-propelled mortar and pestle.

"Nice engine, 27 dragon power. I wish I could have one of those!" thought Feodor, shivering from a sudden gust of wind. Raising his eyes, he saw the storm cloud now directly above him. A heavy shower suddenly drenched him. The carpet was soaked through and losing altitude rapidly. Feodor was only saved because, as he neared the ground, he managed to jump off at the last moment into an opportune haystack.

As he lay there recovering, the rain stopped, and a thick fog spread over the meadow. Feodor thought he could discern through the fog the familiar figure of Dundusa and prepared himself for yet another scolding. Dundusa spoke to him in her familiar nasal voice:

"When I was a young girl, my parents bought a summer cottage with a wonderful garden. In a corner of this garden, horseradish grew wildly with its huge leaves spreading out over everything. Each week I would pull up the leaves, but they would always grow back again. Finally, I decided to *remove the entire root*. I dug a deep hole, but the root was thin, and it broke off. 'Stupid horseradish!' I thought, and left it at that. Through the rest of that summer, no more horseradish leaves appeared, and I forgot about them. Next spring I returned to the summer cottage and was shocked to find five thriving new horseradish plants where the one had grown before. I understood then the necessity of *digging down to the very end of the root*! Otherwise, the horseradish would eventually take over the entire garden. This time I dug down very carefully to where the root system ended, and removed it entirely. In its place I planted an apple tree, which even now produces unheard of bumper crops several times a year."

The fog cleared away, and Feodor thought: "What a bunch of nonsense! I must have hit my head when I fell."

However, Dundusa's reprimand had already entered into his subconscious, and he began to sort through various transportation mishaps which had occurred in his life. It was as if he was sinking deeper and deeper into his past.

Feodor recalled a vivid episode from his childhood. When he was three, his father had given him a scooter. Excited, Feodor rode it down to the road, where he met his neighbor, Grishka, who asked to try it out. Feodor refused and moved on. Then, like a devil out of a snuff box, the hobgoblin Kuzia jumped out onto the roadway and snatched away his scooter. Feodor ran home crying his eyes out and, to make matters worse, his father gave him the belt for what had happened.

"It's too bad I didn't let Grishka have a ride," concluded Feodor. He imagined himself giving the scooter to Grishka, who suggested that they go down to the river to try it out on the steep hill there. Feodor experienced an indescribable *sense of freedom* and speed as he raced down the hill.

Suddenly Feodor heard a strange noise. A Russian stove rose up from behind a nearby haystack. Laying on the stove was an odd-looking fellow in a fur cap.

"Do you want a lift?" he asked.

"Sure, thanks."

"Lie down here. It'll be more fun traveling together."

The stove drifted off out of sight to the sound of balalaikas and heroic singing.

Here is a real-life story of a magician named Varya:

I returned home on the 23rd of February.* My son was drinking wine with his friends. This disturbed me very much, so I began searching my past for an episode when I had been frightened by a drunken man for the very first time. I recalled an incident when I was three years old, in a flash remembering it in great detail. We were waiting at home for our father. My sister was doing her homework, my grand-mother was cooking. Father just wouldn't come home! My grandmother told us that he would probably show up drunk, and she advised us: "You are always hanging all over your daddy, but instead you should say to him: 'Shame on you!' Maybe then he will stop his drinking. The neighbor boy told his father that, and he hasn't been drunk for two weeks!"

Our father finally arrived home and we said exactly what grandmother had told us to say. An argument broke out. Father raised his hand against mother, and she ran away. Then he threw an overcoat at Grandmother to shut her up. My sister said something mean to him and also ran away. I was left all alone, sitting on a chair. Even though I loved

* Red Army Day—in Russia this day is celebrated like Father's Day. [trans]

my father very much, I told him that he was a drunken pig. He rushed at me, threatening to strike me with his hand.

I replayed this scene in my mind but altered it. In the new version, I persuaded Grandmother to bake pies to welcome father when he came home. I began repeating my new name: *"I am the one who welcomes father with pies."* Over time my son stopped carousing with his drinking buddies, and eventually enrolled in college, where he found new friends.

We can analyze this story in the following way. The diagnostic name of Varya is: "I am the one who is troubled by my son's drinking." In order to deal with his drinking problem, she utilizes the technique of *searching for the root*. Varya must recall the first episode in her life when a drunken person disturbed her peace of mind, and then to select a new name to reprogram the root episode. If she is having difficulty finding the root, she can trace back the chain of similar experiences in her life, beginning with the most recent. Gradually, untying knot after knot, she will finally arrive at the first such experience in her life—the root episode. Varya was able to reach that root episode—her father's arrival home drunk when she was three. At that point, she had two methods to choose from.

First method: Varya must *search for an act of thankfulness* associated with the obstacle (her father), which happened at around the same time as the root episode. For example, Varya recalled that once on her father's birthday she had drawn a picture for him which depicted her mother, grandmother, and friends giving him flowers, balloons, and other gifts. Her father was very touched and still today has this picture. This act of thankfulness is incorporated into her formula for soaring: *"I am the one who draws a picture of daddy's birthday."*

Second Method: Varya goes back in her memory to the very threshold of the root episode, when everything was still unclouded, when nothing yet foretold the coming drama. Then she will be able *to reenact the events according to a new script*, sending her father inner peace. The new script states that Varya persuaded her grandmother to bake pies to welcome her father, and this was incorporated into her new name.

This second method of renaming is often utilized by the heroes of the film *Back to the Future*. Varya preferred this method, although both can be equally valuable, depending on the situation. Feodor also used this method when he gave his scooter to Grishka. If it is difficult for you to remember an appropriate act of thankfulness, then apply the *"Back to the Future"* method.

People have a strong belief in the law of cause-and-effect. For this reason, the technique of renaming by searching for the root (the cause) is extremely effective. It is often used in psychotherapy, but apparently is a very ancient method. In the works of Carlos Castaneda, he describes one of the main techniques of don Juan—re-examination, based on researching one's past.

Serge Kahili King, in his book *Urban Shaman*, gives many examples of this technique. He tells an amazing story about a woman in California who severely burnt her leg on the exhaust pipe of a motorcycle. For a long time the burn would not heal, so she started picturing in her mind a different, better scenario in which she did not touch the exhaust pipe, weaving it around in her imagination forty times. The results were very impressive—the severe wound skinned over in only three days. Many of the ideas and techniques in this outstanding book have much in common with our own world view.

In neuro-linguistic programming (NLP), a similar technique is widely utilized called "changing one's personal history." Recently in Russia the idea of karma, thanks largely to the works of Sergey Nikolaevich Lazarev, has begun to penetrate into the mass consciousness. The technique of renaming by searching for the root, which, in fact, alters karma, is gradually becoming better understood and accepted. Also, various methods for renaming by searching for the root are fundamental to Holodynamics and Dianetics.

The effective use of this technique of searching for the root is based on the fact that, as a rule, a person can recall vivid scenes from his own life while plunging deeply into childhood memories. We experience once again those intense emotions which only a child can feel.

Following are some guidelines for those who wish to use this technique of renaming to work with clients.* First, the person must clearly state the issue at hand. Next, the client seeks out an earlier episode in life which is similar to the current issue and, continuing to trace the chain of similar experiences back in memory, finally discovers the root episode. This root episode is considered the primary cause of the issue which is currently manifesting in the client's life. Generally, root episodes occur in early childhood. In order to help a person *remember the root*, you can try narrating stories showing how others have *recalled* root episodes. Sometimes, following established practice, you can narrate several stories, inserting one into the other (the so-called spiral of Milton Erickson). An example of working in this way is described in the story narrated in the second section called "This is no way to treat a pregnant woman!"

The question is often asked: What should I do if I can't remember the root episode? There are various options: stubbornly keep trying until you finally discover the unfortunate event; remember a similar episode and proclaim it the root; or switch to a different technique.

* The techniques described in this book can be used for resolving the issues of others. Many examples of working with clients are contained in the magical stories given in the second section.

Renaming the Actual Obstacle

"Every single thing's crooked," Alice thought to herself, "and she's all over pins!"

"May I put your shawl straight for you?" she added aloud, "...and dear me, what a state your hair is in!"

Alice carefully released the brush, and did her best to get the hair into order.

Lewis Carroll—*Alice through the Looking Glass*

Feodor and Emelia rode along on top of the stove.

"How can I possibly find my princess?" Feodor asked.

"What the hell do you need her for?"

"I'm in love with Frosia. The world is nothing to me without her," he replied.

Seeing that Feodor was imprisoned by yet another illusion, the wise magician understood that it was too early to accept him as his apprentice.

"At least I can teach him to work with the actual obstacle," thought Emelia.

"Take this path, Feodor. It will lead you to a palace which is not a palace, and a cottage which is not a cottage. There you will find that which no one knows. If you can manage to take that with you, it will help you find your princess.

Feodor embraced Emelia, climbed down from the stove, and set off down the path. It led him to a small cottage with no windows or porch. He entered stealthily and hid behind the stove. Suddenly, a dwarf with a long beard walked into the cottage and shouted:

"My friend, Khron! I'm hungry!"

Out of nowhere a table appeared laden with a barrel of beer and a roasted bull with a sharp knife stuck in its side. The dwarf sat down at the table, pulled out the knife, and began slicing the meat, dipping each piece in garlic before eating it; he was thoroughly enjoying his meal. He finished off the roast to the last bone while drinking down the entire barrel of beer.

He commanded: "My friend, Khron! Clear the table!" The table instantly disappeared as if it had never existed.

Feodor stayed in hiding until the dwarf left. Stepping out from behind the stove, he gathered up his courage and called out:

"My friend, Khron! Feed me!"

Out of nowhere a table appeared laden with various dishes, appetizers, desserts, and various wines and meads. Feodor sat at the table and said:

"My friend, Khron! Come sit down with me! Let's eat and drink together."

An invisible voice replied:

"Thank you, my good man. How many years have I served here and yet have never been offered so much as a burnt crust, but you have invited me to share your meal."

Feodor looked around and wondered: "No one is visible, and yet food is vanishing piece by piece from the table. The wines and meads are pouring themselves; the goblet gallops around all by itself."

"My friend, Khron! Show yourself to me!"

"That's impossible; no one can see me. I am that which no one knows."

"My friend, Khron! Would you like to be my servant?"

"Why not? I see that you're a kind person."

And they went away together.

The technique of searching for the root, as elucidated in the previous section, compels us to delve deeply into our past. It is sometimes easier, though, to apply instead a technique we call *renaming the actual obstacle*. This technique is illustrated in the following story told by Andrey. It depicts a typical example of working with the actual obstacle.

One night I was driving my family home and inadvertently ran a stoplight. It was very late, when there are no cars and, more important, no traffic cops. So I was completely surprised when an officer with a striped baton appeared out of nowhere. He signaled for me to stop. He looked frozen stiff, standing there alone in his thin boots. There was a heavy frost outside, and the officer was unconsciously tapping out a dance with his feet, which were obviously freezing! In my mind I offered him a glass of vodka, then hot tea with honey, and, to top it off, heavy boots trimmed with reindeer fur. At that very moment, the officer—royal knight of urban crosswalks—relaxed his forehead, and the stern furrows crossing his brow smoothed over. I started repeating to myself: *"I am the one who gives boots to the royal knight of urban crosswalks."* He let me off with hardly a slap on the wrist.

In this technique you first study the obstacle, and then mentally offer various acts which "improve"* that obstacle. If the obstacle is immediately "improved" as a result of your mental gift, then you have found the correct renaming formula. If the obstacle is not "improved," or has even "worsened" (not likely), you then just pretend that it actually was "improved" and compose a formula for soaring.

---

* Quotation marks signify that the improvements which I strive for are *based on the assumptions of my personal world view.*

Renaming by Finding the Ray of Light

When you look into the ashes, look well.
Deepak Chopra—*The Way of the Wizard*

If you find yourself in darkness, and all you see is one pale ray of light, you must walk straight toward it, without speculating whether or not there is any sense in it. Perhaps there really is no sense in it, but certainly there is no sense to just sit in the darkness.
Victor Pelevin—*Hermit and Six-Toes*

Feodor turned to his invisible companion:

"Please help me find my princess, my friend Khron."

"There is a certain very old frog, who knows where to find her. She has lived in the bogs for three hundred years. Go seek her out, but without me, as there is nothing there for me. I have an aunt who lives in a kingdom far, far away. She is a sensitive woman, and just today she sent me a telepathic message, asking me to visit her. Release me, Feodor, but if you should need me, call out my name, and I will find you."

"Go, my friend Khron."

Feodor set off for the Lower Vargun Bog. This was much easier said than done. He wandered around lost for a long time, or was it a short time? Finally he reached the bog and called out:

"Grandmother Frog! Are you alive?"

"I am alive."

"Please come out to me from the bog."

The old frog slowly crawled out of the bog.

"Do you know where I can find the Princess Frosia?"

"Once I could show you the way, but now I'm so old. I can no longer leap very far, and a River of Fire blocks the way. No animal can leap over it, nor bird fly over it. Only I could cross it, when I was a young COMSOMOL* member, but now I can't."

"Tell me more about yourself. You must have seen much in your long life."

"I have been starving for many years, and all my strength is lost. But there once was a time when I'd bathe myself in warm milk which would rejuvenate me, and then I could jump all the way to the edge of the world. But where can I get milk now? Hopping to the village would be the death of me."

Feodor went to the village, found a cow, and brought back a pail of milk. He set Grandmother Frog in it and brought her to the River of Fire. At its edge, Feodor took Grandmother Frog out of the pail and set her on the ground.

"Now, dear friend, sit down on my back," she commanded

"What are you saying, Grandmother? You're so small. I'll squash you!"

"Don't worry, you won't squash me. Just sit down and hold on tight."

Feodor mounted Grandmother Frog and she began to swell up. She grew bigger and bigger until she was as large as a haystack.

"Are you holding on tight?"

---

* COMSOMOL is the Young Communist League, a mass youth group during the Soviet Era. [trans]

"Yes, Grandmother."

She continued to swell up bigger and bigger until she was larger than the dark forest. And then how she leaped! She sailed high over the River of Fire.

"Now, Feodor, we are on the island Buyan. From here the princess is only a stone's throw away."

We will now examine yet another world view, which correlates with the principle of duality popular in the East known as "Yin and Yang." Within any object you can find a creative element, and within every destructive phenomenon there exists a spark of life—the *ray of light*. For example, a tree which is withering yet still has powerful roots, or a mangy dog which still leads the pack.

The technique of renaming by finding the ray of light is simple: I locate this ray, the source of strength, and it leads me to success. In our examples, you might compose names like these: *"I am the one who grows powerful roots,"* and *"I am the one who leads the pack."* The following story told by a magician illustrates how this translates into real life.

I was on the subway. Sitting at the back of the car were two filthy homeless guys in torn coats carrying wooden walking sticks. But each held in his hands a very thick book which they were fully engrossed in. At the next stop, another homeless fellow entered and moved through the car begging for money. He looked terrible. Not only was he dirty, but he was also injured. He had a black eye, and there were several cuts on his bloodied shaven head. He stopped in front of me and, without thinking twice, I gave him some money.

The two other vagrants began discussing loudly how life was no easier for them, but nobody ever gave them money, and they would never fall so low as to beg. I realized that I had taken their bait, they had aroused my pity. There were very few people on the car, but their ruckus was irritating everyone, and some people told them to settle down. Instantly I saw the ray of light—they were homeless but were reading, and what thick books! In my mind I spoke the name: *"I am the one who is reading a very thick book."* The car became quiet. The injured fellow stopped begging for money and squatted down by the doors, and the two others opened their books to continue reading.

Imaginative Renaming

Alice looked all round her at the flowers and the blades of grass, but she could not see anything that looked like the right thing to eat or drink under the circumstances. There was a large mushroom growing near her, about the same height as herself; and, when she had looked under it, and on both sides of it, and behind it, it occurred to her that she might as well look and see what was on top of it. She stretched herself up on tiptoe, and peeped over the edge of the mushroom, and her eyes immediately met those of a large blue caterpillar that was sitting on the top, with its arms folded, quietly smoking a long hookah, and taking not the smallest notice of her or of anything else.

Lewis Carroll—*Alice's Adventures in Wonderland*

If you have imagination as a grain of sesame seed... all things are possible to you.

Richard Bach—*Illusions*

Meanwhile, the princess was languishing in captivity, and dark thoughts crowded her mind:

"What if no one rescues me? Will the best years of my life be wasted in this hole?"

Water dripped monotonously from the ceiling of the cave and, hypnotized by the sound, the princess fell into a deep sleep.

She dreamed that she was found by a terrifying, hunch-backed beast with crooked arms, claws, and hooves. He had a hooked nose, long fangs protruding from his mouth, and was completely covered in hair. Frosia started shouting hysterically and frantically waved her small, white hands in the air.

"Now I'll have to endure a long life of suffering married to this horrible beast! I'd rather throw myself under a speeding train than live with that thing!"

The princess lay there grief-stricken for some time, but there was nothing else to do—the wedding was set for the following day. She decided to try to improve her attitude: "Could there possibly be anything about him I could ever love?"

She took a closer look at the beast and noticed that he had kind eyes. They were shining with an inner smile, and those eyes began to hypnotize Frosia. The beast transformed first into a shining cocoon, then into a New Russian. He was dressed in a crimson-colored tuxedo with gold buttons, lots of gold chains and rings, and a fashionable, spiky haircut. With a victorious shout "Bonsai!" she threw her arms around the neck of the former beast, and kissed him passionately with her sugary lips. Then the second transfiguration happened. The new Russian turned into a hero more handsome than could be described in any fairytale, or by any pen. The princess woke up and the handsome hero of her dream was standing there by her side. Of course, it was Feodor.

Let's say an obstacle rises up before me—my wife is furious and threatening me with an iron skillet. I immediately compose an internal movie—for instance, a Centaur selling sunflower seeds at the marketplace. Then I choose a name: *"I am a Centaur who sells roasted sunflower seeds."*

Magicians prefer to imagine new, even extraordinary movies, which usually do not have analogues in the common world view—a Centaur as a sunflower seed vendor.

I *consciously create* this movie myself, not waiting for an image to just appear. Usually this happens very quickly, although sometimes it seems that the internal pictures exist in and of themselves, that I "see" them.

Many magicians have their own personal method for creating imaginary pictures. Some shut their eyes, so as not to be disturbed by their surroundings. Sparks, dots, stripes, and patches of color float through their internal sight, coalescing into familiar images—people, wild animals, cars... One of our friends prefers to think up images while looking at objects sideways. don Juan suggests defocusing the glance (c.f. the works of Carlos Castaneda).

Following are two examples of imaginative renaming:

Every evening for many years I could clearly hear through my walls my elderly neighbors drinking heavily with their friends. They would get completely smashed! I dreaded each evening and had trouble falling asleep. My repeated complaints to the police brought no results.

One day I went to a seminar on magic and became acquainted with the technique of imaginative renaming, which I decided to apply to my problem. Starting with the drunken voices resounding in my head, I imagined a thick Chinese crayon. One half of the crayon was blue, and the other half red. In my mind I sharpened the red half of the crayon and heard the name: *"I am the one who is sharpening the red end of the crayon."* To my utter amazement, the drunken revelry ended that very night. My neighbors had simply stopped drinking.

One evening my husband Pavel dragged into the house a whole slew of electronic components and tried to put them together into a computer. After some time, he burst into the room, yelling: "Don't even come near me! Nothing's working out!"

Usually I would be completely crushed by his comments, but this time I imagined that *I was basking on the hot sand on a sun-drenched desert island.*

I felt relief from this picture but still harbored doubts deep in my heart: "What if nothing works out for Pavel, and that horrible scene happens again?" I went into the kitchen, poured a whole pile of semolina onto a plate, and put it in the microwave. After several minutes, I pulled out the plate and stuck my hands into the warm "sand."

My son came in, asking: "What're you doing?"

I answered: "Warming my hands."

He came up and started playing with the semolina and, inspired and invigorated, I decided to iron the linen. My mood was remarkably good, and I completely forgot that my husband was angry. Pavel again entered the room. He had calmed down somewhat and, stating that it still wasn't working out, he immediately withdrew. I remembered *basking on the hot sand.* As I continued ironing, Pavel stepped once more into the room and, with complete calm, stated: "You know, nothing is going right today. Let's have some tea together."

Pavel didn't work on the computer any more that day, but his mood was fine. The next day Pavel bought some more components, and the computer started working.

Support Signals

It became completely quiet all around. The flowers
sprung up. And the Divine Gnome fluttered from flower to
flower, collecting sweet nectar in a green, enameled mug.
"We drink to our victory in grievous battle!" he proclaimed cheerfully and in a single gulp drained the mug.

Evgeny Kliuev—*Between Two Chairs*

If I watch for *support signals*—auspicious events which occur
around me—this signifies that I am in harmony. Whatever I do
will turn out well, I see success and happiness everywhere I turn.
The following narrative shows a chain of support signals.

I had just walked up to the traffic signal *as the green
light came on*. I crossed the street, and right away *a half-
empty bus rolled up*, which took me to the subway station.
I descended to the platform, and directly in front of me
the train doors flew open. In the subway car, I immediately
found an empty seat, and *an elegant woman with a bouquet
of spectacular roses* sat down opposite me. At the subway
exit, a young man, *smiling broadly*, stepped forward *with
arms outspread to greet the woman*. On the street, I saw *a
man whirling around in a rousing dance* to the pleasure of
a crowd of spectators. From the loudspeaker, which hung
on the building wall a few yards from the dancer, a song
blared out: *"You shall have all that you desire..."*

It was obvious that everything would turn out well for me that day.

Because I was in a state of soaring, *my plans and projects were realized*, my wishes were fulfilled. Consciousness of oneself as a magician creates the conditions required so that all life's needs happen of themselves. Only time is required to draw success to me. And if it doesn't come immediately, I won't fall into despair.

There is a well-known Indian parable:

Once Shiva came down to earth. There he saw a holy Brahman, who for his entire life had endured the harshest asceticism and observed all the rituals, constantly praying to Shiva. The Brahman asked the Three-Eyed One:

"Oh, Mahadeva, when will I attain enlightenment?"

"You have only one incarnation left."

At these words, the Brahman became furious and started cursing Shiva, insisting that he had already earned enlightenment in this life. With these words, the Brahman no doubt extended his term of confinement in human form for many more lifetimes.

Next Shiva passed by a tipsy peasant who was making love to another man's wife. The peasant asked the Six-Armed One:

"Oh, Mahadeva, when will I attain enlightenment?"

"You still have ten incarnations to go."

The peasant, wild with joy, broke into a dance, singing ecstatically: "And in the end I will be free!"

At that moment he attained enlightenment.

Transfiguration

"It's possible to insist, to properly insist, even though we know that what we're doing is useless," he said, smiling. "But we must know first that our acts are useless and yet we must proceed as if we didn't know it. That's a sorcerer's controlled folly." ...

I asked him if controlled folly meant that his acts were never sincere but were only the acts of an actor.

"My acts are sincere," he said, "but they are only the acts of an actor."

"Then everything you do must be controlled folly!" I said truly surprised.

"Yes, everything," he said.

Carlos Castaneda—*A Separate Reality*

Feodor took the princess by the hand. They emerged from the cave and set out for the River of Fire. Smitten by exultation, they were not watching their steps, and they stumbled into a trap—a pit covered over with branches. At that moment, an alarm went off.

Frightened by the snapping branches and shrill scream of the high-tech, imported alarm system, a wild mustang galloped past the pit, neighing impetuously and stomping its hooves. Feodor jumped onto all fours and began mimicking the stallion, whinnying enthusiastically and prancing about the pit. He gradually worked himself into a frenzy and started pawing at the ground with his right hind leg, shod in a heavy tarpaulin boot from the factory "Quickwalker."

Frosia, worried about her fiance's mental state, goggled at his escapades in speechless amazement. The "mustang" froze momentarily: "What're you starin' at, babe? C'mon, help me out here; pretend you're a horse. That was a sign from above—stalking is gonna save us."

Bursting into laughter, Frosia threw her front "legs" around Feodor's neck and rubbed her luxurious mane against him.

A minute later Feodor and Frosia were pulled out of the hole in triumph by three demons. Before Feodor could become alarmed, he recognized one of them as his old acquaintance.

"Hey, aren't you the one I helped split up the gold?"

"Ha! It's Solomon! Come have fun with us."

"Thanks, guys, but first I must bring happiness to a grieving old man—I have to deliver Frosia to her father."

"That's easy for us to do!"

That very instant Feodor and Frosia were transported to the palace. The king was overwhelmed with joy, and he immediately arranged a feast in their honor for all the world to share. It's true, I swear, for I was there.

According to the traditions of some Native North American tribes, a vision or revelation received in dreams or during prayer was crucial to one's life.[*] The fate of individuals and the tribe was predetermined by what was revealed. When coming of age, boys in the Oglala tribes sought their personal vision in the "mourning ritual." They were sent far away from camp, where in solitude they fasted and prayed for four days

---

[*] Information cited in this and subsequent paragraphs comes from the books *Black Elk Speaks* by John Neihardt and *The Sacred Pipe* by Joseph Epes Brown.

straight. Next, they performed a purification ritual in the traditional Native American sweat lodge, after which they were left for the night inside a "magic circle," where the seeker wept and prayed, beseeching the Great Spirit for instruction.

A major part of the revelation was a spirit protector which appeared in the form of an animal, bird, or sometimes an object or a mystical person. According to the content of his dreams, the seeker might be given, for instance, the name of "a spirited horse," and the spirit protector in the form of a horse would watch over him in days of war and peace. Whoever received a particularly impressive vision became the shaman and developed a Great Vision over the course of his entire life. The shaman healed the people, regulated the weather, ensured the hunt, etc., by portraying various personages from his vision. It was believed that the Great Vision became stronger when reproduced in the presence of members of the tribe. This performance in humorous form was acted out by special Indian clowns—the Heyoka; indeed, it was believed that the sacred strength could penetrate most deeply into a person only while laughing.

Some magicians also like to utilize certain "classic" internal movies (cf. "The Frog Princess" and "Changing Reflections"), while others prefer to create new and different movies each time. The process by which these movies are created is known as transfiguration.

If an obstacle rises up in front of me, it means that I am no longer in a state of soaring; I have forgotten that I am a magician. The solution to this is simple—I must regain my status as a magician. I look around me for the *support signals*, including those not connected in any way to the obstacle.

Suppose I am experiencing difficulties in business, and my worries give me no peace. Entering the kitchen, I hear a radio broadcast: "If you feed your chickens 'Riabushka' multivitamins, they will lay up to 20 eggs per month." Or I run into a homeless person, whose shabby coat full of holes has been painstakingly repaired with Scotch tape. I compose a formula for soaring. *"I am a laying hen which pecks 'Riabushka' multivitamins"* or *"I am the one who painstakingly repairs my coat with Scotch tape."* Without delay, I start repeating it. By affirming the magical formula, I receive support signals which confirm my status as a magician. Thus, having begun *"to repair my coat,"* I can take note of the man carrying on his shoulders a little girl with a blue balloon, and so forth. The sequence of positive signals very quickly brings me back to a state of soaring.

Like the Heyoka, I creatively personify a new role. For example, scattering vitamin pills on the floor and squatting, I "peck" the miraculous peas with loud clucking.

By embodying the success formula, I return to a state of soaring, and the situation is by itself resolved, often in a completely unexpected way. For instance, from my diligent pecking at the "Riabushka" vitamins, a telephone call may distract me. It is a friend with a lucrative proposal.

Following are actual stories illustrating transfiguration:

When I arrived home from work one evening, my wife said: "Your mother called. She was throwing up all day with a temperature of 102." A few minutes later, I heard my wife laughing loudly at the comedy show she was watching, so I glanced over at the television. The screen showed that favorite hero of young boys, Hulk Hogan, dressed up in a pink tutu. This was an obvious support signal, and I composed an appropriate formula for soaring: *"I am the wrestler who dances ballet in a pink tutu."* The next morning my mother called to tell me that late last night she finally got some relief. Her temperature suddenly dropped, and her

nausea went away. As it turned out, this happened immediately after I performed the transfiguration.

As mentioned earlier, you should, like the Heyoka, *act out* the
movie which corresponds to your formula for soaring, which
allows you *to embody it in life*. This is what magicians do.

I was very nervous that my daughter Anya kept coming home late. At a magician's seminar, I had received the
name: *"I am the swan maiden with a lace collar and a propeller on my head, who wanders around a clearing in the forest
with a little boy."*
Returning home that evening, I saw a light on in the
kitchen. Could my daughter be home already? And so
it was. I came in excited and announced to everyone: "I .
need a propeller and a lace collar." The children rushed in
to help, and we constructed a propeller out of cardboard.
Anya, wanting to do something nice for me, decided to
bake nut pastries. She ran down to the supermarket for
sour cream, mixed the ingredients, and started kneading
the dough.
Stepping into the kitchen wearing the collar and propeller, I asked: "Anya, why are you home early?"
"I'm done partying," she replied.
The next day after the seminar, I arrived home late. A
note was lying on the table from my jealous partner: "It's
all over; I'm leaving you. But you'll still have to answer to
me!" Right then, he showed up and began yelling at me,
wanting to know where I'd been all day.
I proclaimed: "I am a swan maiden with a propeller on
my head."
"You can't get to me that way! I don't believe in that
nonsense!"

I went out to attach the propeller to the top of my head and appeared silently before him. He immediately tore up the note and handed me a piece of chocolate.

✦

By embodying the magical name, taking on an unusual, humorous role, I break down standard stereotypes. At that moment, I am a happy and free being, conscious of the illusory nature of my personality. Really, a person wearing a propeller on her head just can't have any problems!

Embodying a comical image is an *original, absurd ritual.* I perform the humorous ritual with all seriousness—at least as much as I am capable of—meticulously elaborating each detail. For example, I might make a propeller which whirls as I walk.

Nowadays, the creation and performance of absurd rituals ·has become an independent technique. While preparing and performing a ritual, I do not have to compose a formula *"I am the one who..."* It is naturally present in the ritual.

You might get the impression from this book that the magician takes action only when he faces a problem. This is not always so. The magician often creates and performs absurd rituals without any goal at all. Once someone proposed this ritual during a seminar on magic: at noontime, take a child's cap gun and a pennant to a traffic signal. When the light changes to yellow, raise the pistol and pennant upwards. When it turns green, shoot off the pistol, wave the pennant, and call out: "Vorschmack!"

Many participants at the seminar enjoyed performing this ritual, altering various details according to their own taste— one switched the pistol to a whistle, another to a sparkler, and so on.

Renaming on the Wing

I'm the lantern that keeps burning dimly at night,
I'm the cricket that sits on the furnace so bright,
I'm the blind whose smooth breast hides the light of the moon,
I'm the snoring that drives silence out of the room.

I'm the pen which allows you to write lines in stride,
I'm the note or the letter which lies to one side,
I'm the hosepipe with languid bliss coated,
I'm the rustle of leaves barely noted.*

Following is a story by a certain magician we know:

I was preparing for a job interview. It had been overcast
all day, but when I left my house, the sun was just peeping
out. On the subway, my attention was drawn to a fancily
dressed woman. *An inscrutable smile floated across her face,
and something fluffy—like a fox's tail but canary-colored—cir-
cled around her neck. Knitted gloves dangled from the sleeves
of her lavender jacket.* Emerging onto the street, I admired
the *bright, blue sky with a few wispy clouds rose-tinted by the
setting sun.* Based on these support signals, I concluded
that the interview would go well, and that the work would
prove to be a perfect fit for me. And so it turned out.

* This poem was translated by John Woodsworth. [trans]

An unbroken chain of support signals rising before me confirms that I am in a state of soaring. If not, I can enter the state by using the simple technique of *renaming on the wing*. I begin by *continuously* composing new formulas for soaring by noticing the pleasing and amusing scenes around me. I find something good in everything occuring within my field of vision.

For example, in the story just cited, I could compose a sequence of names: *"I am the sun peeping out," "I smile inscrutably," "I am a fluffy, canary-colored tail circling around a neck," "I am knitted gloves dangling from the sleeves of a lavender jacket," "I am the one who rose-tints the wispy clouds high up in the blue sky."* While renaming on the wing, I quickly enter into a state of soaring. If at the same time I also *embody* that name into my entire being—that is, I portray physically the sun peeping out, the furry tail circling a neck, etc.—then the result can be stunning. The following story illustrates the technique of renaming on the wing.

My friend Valeria, who trusts my taste, asked me to help her choose a nightstand to match her furniture. So one morning, she and her husband picked me up in their car. We drove all over Samara, but we could not find an acceptable piece anywhere.

I began renaming on the wing. I immediately noticed a sign advertising: "You know, everything will happen in time!" I composed the name: *"I am that which you know will happen in time!"* I saw a sign for the Department of Motor Vehicles: "Every child on the road is your own!" I became *"someone else's child who's never on the road."* Next, I saw a woman in a fur coat carrying a pink makeup bag. A tiny kitten was scampering after her . It looked comical, and I said to myself: *"I am a pink makeup bag in a fur coat walking a kitten."* I saw a dog curled up asleep in a cardboard box: *"I am the one who is sleeping in a cardboard box."* I experienced an inexpressible happiness from all this, noticing only the positive signals, which were striking in their uniqueness. It was as if I were a relay wand being passed from one signal to the next.

When we drove by one particular store, I felt like going in and asked my friends to stop the car. Right at the entryway, I caught sight of the curtains of my dreams, and at a very low price. I had long been planning to redecorate my bedroom with new curtains, but I only had three hundred rubles on me; they cost a thousand. Unable to let go, I thought: "Wait a minute, I'm a magician!" I noticed a delicate tassel dangling down from "my" curtains, so I renamed myself as *"a tassel adorning the curtains."*

I'm not sure why I went up to the second floor, where automobile parts were sold. There I met my dear friend Vasya, whom I had not seen for three years. We hugged each other warmly, and he said: "Please forgive me. I called you several times to repay you the money I borrowed, but I just couldn't ever get ahold of you."

"What do you mean? What money?"

"Don't you remember? We were going to Natasha's birthday party, and you lent me money to buy her a present."

I finally did recall the present we bought her, and also that I paid Vasya's share. Vasya quickly converted the debt into dollars at the rate of three years ago, multiplied it by today's rate, and announced an astronomical sum which he promised to pay back immediately.

"I'd rather borrow it from you for now; I don't have enough cash on me for the curtains."

"C'mon, let's go. I'll buy them for you."

Altogether Vasya gave me seven hundred rubles, and I left the store with the package under my arm. Valeria was staggered. I was exhilarated, though, and continued renaming on the wing. Suddenly, right in front of me was an astounding sight: an old man smiling from ear to ear, his gray beard fluttering in the wind, wearing a black cap and a priest's robe with a blue jacket over it, and skis (!) under his arm. "Could I be dreaming?" I asked myself. Valeria was talking to her husband, so they didn't even notice this amazing spectacle.

At the time we were passing by a department store, and I noticed an advertisement on the corner: "Furniture for sale, enter next right." For no apparent reason, I blurted out: "That store has the perfect nightstand for you!"

As we were parking, I thought: "What if I'm wrong? What will I say if they don't have any?"

Entering the store, we immediately saw two inlaid nightstands in oak veneer. They were still being sold at old prices, so instead of the seven thousand rubles my friends expected to pay, they cost only three. You can only imagine the astonished looks they gave me.

Let's turn our attention to the name: *"I am that which you know will happen in time!"* Such a name is constructed on the basis of an ingenious principle used by ancient bards: "I sing what I see."

The idea of renaming on the wing is wonderfully expressed in the poetry of the magician Petr Dmitryev:

> I am the cold and wintry day,
> To north winds I give no resistance.
> I am the stout old stump and stay
> There sticking out with firm persistence.
>
> For lovers I am the secluded
> Corner in the garden haven.

I am the huge (with leaves protruding)
Maple with its helpful raven.

I am that raven's excrement,
And hurl myself with inspiration
On a flight of welcoming intent—
A hat serves as my landing station.

I hide a languid gaze as a narrow
And foxy eyelash—yes, that's me,
I love to chase the wayward sparrow:
I'm just a happy chickadee.

I am a big old garbage-can
I am the useless trash within it.
A chicken-rib is what I am—
A mangy cat comes gnawing on it.

I am its purring, still, sublime,
On knees so huge they're simply frightful.
I am a flask of Georgian wine,
To drink me is a taste delightful.

I am the moon with stately head
So bright amidst the sky all darkening.
I am the cockroach on white bread,
The ravenous plague, to all disheartening.

I am the paving stone dejected,
On which fine steeds may trot clip-clop.
I am the glove, perfume-infected,
Which ladies sometimes will let drop.

I am the bright green traffic light
On a road with dusty incrustations,
A motor-car revving with all its might
As I speed to hidden destinations.*

Following is the author's experience of the day's events reflecting this poem:

Waking up, I open the curtains and look outside. The day is cold and windy. My glance falls on a dog running around a huge tree stump. On level with the window, a raven sits perched on a branch. Below it, a girl in an old-fashioned bonnet walks past... I catch sight of a chickadee stealing breadcrumbs from a sparrow.

I gather my things and head downstairs to the entryway, scaring off a couple of lovebirds hiding in a secluded nook. Right then, a spry old woman overtakes me carrying her trash can (in our building there are no garbage chutes). Walking out onto the street, I notice a mangy old cat gnawing a chicken bone. I imagine the cat purring on the old woman's lap as she gently strokes its fur.

There is an empty wine bottle next to the trash bin and a stale crust of bread. I imagine the joy a cockroach must feel when it happens upon such a hefty slice of bread—a hearty meal! I recall eating such a piece of bread yesterday evening, sitting in the kitchen admiring the moon.

I warm up the car and drive off. Alongside the road, a huge billboard depicting a horse attracts my attention. This brings to mind a horse's hooves clattering over the cobblestones. Later on, I catch sight of a glove fallen onto the pavement. Straight ahead a green traffic light emerges out of the gloom...

---

* This poem was translated by John Woodsworth. [trans]

Testing the Waters

"What you saw was not an agreement from the world," he said. "Crows flying or cawing are never an agreement. That was an omen!"

"An omen of what?"

"A very important indication about you," he replied cryptically.

At that very instant the wind blew the dry branch of a bush right to our feet.

"That was an agreement!" he exclaimed and looked at me with shiny eyes and broke into a belly laugh...

"This is very weird," I said, "but I feel really good."

I heard the cawing of a crow in the distance. He lifted his finger to his right ear and smiled.

"That was an omen," he said.

A small rock tumbled downhill and made a crashing sound when it landed in the chaparral. He laughed out loud and pointed his finger in the direction of the sound.

"And that was an agreement," he said.

Carlos Castaneda—*Journey to Ixtlan*

When I set a goal, a corresponding internal movie is launched. I then witness the process of achieving that goal in the outer world, often in a modified form. By observing the events (the *signs*) unfolding around me, I can determine what kind of effort, and how much, will be required to secure the desired result.

An unfavorable sign, in the form of an obstacle, portends potential difficulties in achieving the goal. The easier it is to remove an obstacle, the less time and effort will be necessary.

Suppose someone calls me to propose that I buy a large shipment of flour at a favorable price. While I'm talking, *my coffee boils over*. After the phone call, as I'm cleaning the stove, I tip over the coffeepot spilling the leftover coffee, which settles into *an aromatic puddle* in the middle of the kitchen floor. Frustrated and angry, I suddenly "see the light"—I realize the source of the trouble, and decide to turn down the deal to purchase the flour. In the end, another friend purchases it and suffers a huge loss.

Another example: I am invited to a business meeting. Before leaving my house, I hear on the television the following commercial:

"Today is a *critical day* for me, so I can't go roller skating with you."

"You should try *Always* sanitary pads."

"Now that I use Always *sanitary pads, I can go roller skating any day I want, not that I'm all that good a skater."*

I understand from the commercial that this is a critical day for me; it would be pointless for me to go to the meeting. But the ad also communicates that, if I go to the meeting carrying these magical sanitary pads, then success will be assured. What's more, I can go at any time. The end of the commercial tells me that there is still much for me to learn. So I buy a pack of sanitary pads and take them with me to the meeting, which turns out very successfully.

If I observe the support signals—"agreements from the world," as don Juan puts it—it means that my plan is patterned after that of all creation. However modest, it becomes part of the greater plan of Nature. Once I was planning a business trip to Samara and went to buy my ticket. At the cashier's window, there was one person ahead of me, who bought a ticket... to Samara! The business trip exceeded all my expectations.

When faced with a difficult choice, I first *test the waters*. Suppose I can't decide whether to sell an apartment now or to wait. Noticing a raven perched on a tree outside my window, I assign it the role of arbiter: if in the next 27 seconds the raven defecates, then I should sell the apartment immediately; if it takes longer, then I'd better wait; if the raven flies away or doesn't show any inclination to defecate, then I shouldn't sell the apartment at all. I have hardly established these conditions in my mind, when the raven poops. I know then that I can start selling the apartment right away without worrying, knowing that the transaction will proceed quickly and profitably.

People throughout the ages have always tested the waters using various means. This process is really just another form of divination—like reading animal entrails, clouds, cards, runes, coins, daisies, etc. Magicians approach divination creatively, devising extraordinary methods for testing the waters.

I had to go to the pharmacy to buy some medicine. They were out at the store near my home, so I walked to the bus stop thinking: "If a bus comes, I will walk in that direction, but if a trolley comes, then that other direction." At that moment, an express bus raced past me, so I followed it in a third direction. Soon I found a pharmacy, which had the medicine at the old prices—in fact, at half-price!

The result of testing the waters does not necessarily give a final verdict. When something attracts me, but signs warn me of difficulties, I can face these difficulties directly and play the renaming game. As the saying goes: "Desire makes the impossible—possible." In any good short story, film, or play, the hero always overcomes a series of obstacles, which forms the basic plot of the work. This often gives people the impression that the purpose of life consists of constantly surmounting hurtles and passing through various hardships. We do not share this point of view—we enjoy living with ease, not tangling ourselves up in plans which only create problems for ourselves and others.

Note:

The authors do not accept claims like this:

"I tested the waters as described in your book but in the end had to 'muddle through a puddle.' I challenge you to a duel!"

By this very assertion, the plaintiff has renounced his power as a magician, attempting to shift the responsibility for his behavior onto Uncle Vasya. The art of testing the waters, like all the techniques given in this book, requires practice.

Retelling in "I"

At exactly the wrong moment, I become confused and frightened; I feel weak, indifferent, and want to cower away, shrivel up into nothing, be totally inconspicuous, and just fall asleep.

"Monologue of an Impotent Man"
Ernest Tsvetkov—*Master of Self-knowledge or Immersion into "I"*

This section examines a very simple, effective method for resolving problems. Let's say I have a conflict with some person. I describe this conflict in detail, but instead of my adversary's name, and appropriate pronouns, I insert "I" and "me." As a magician, I know that I create my own world; everything around me is an extension of myself. Therefore, I can honestly proclaim my true "archenemy"—myself. Following is a conversation between a husband and wife altered in this manner.

"Why did I get home so late?"
"What? I think I was out with other women? I was doing business."
"What sort of business was I up to after eleven?"
"That's none of my business! I wouldn't ask me, what I'm up to after work, and what I was doing there with my sick drug addicts."
"Maybe the next time I come home I won't be here!"

"Then maybe I won't threaten me."

"I'm finished with me."

"Actually, it's me that's finished with me! I'm out of here."

"And I don't have to come back."

"This is all my fault."

"No, it's my fault. Come let me kiss me."

"I really should give me more attention, spend more time with me."

This is a monologue of a mother arriving home from work, as written by her son.

I arrive home from work and ask me: "What have I been eating? Only fruit? And who do I do all this cooking for? Myself? Is it really so hard for me to warm up the meal I cooked for me? And did I do my homework? I forgot to take notes? What was I thinking? I really couldn't have just called me? I went to the movies? What else did I do? Was I really sitting at the computer all day? And why am I glued to the floor? Did I eat a watermelon, or something? Of course, I couldn't bother washing the dishes. I'd rather wait until I get home from work to fight with me? Do I really think I like fighting with me, like some psychotic? I'm really not such a bad person. I sorted out that mess on the balcony—something I wouldn't expect of me.

In the very process of writing out monologues and dialogues, the wall separating me from my adversary collapses of itself. The absurdity of it all becomes clear, how ridiculous confrontation really is—*I am doing battle against myself.* As I retell events in *"I,"* there are times when I can't tell from whose point of view the monologue is written, even what is really happening. Usually relationships quickly return to normal after retelling in *I*. If it doesn't work right away, you can try repeating key or humorous phrases in the monologue until the conflict is finally resolved.

You can apply this method to settle any issue. Once Svetlana lost the key to her apartment. She didn't want to spend the money for a duplicate, since she knew that somewhere she had spares. So, instead, Svetlana had to constantly make arrangements with her daughter as to who should take the key, causing her much inconvenience. After attending a seminar in magic, Svetlana retold the situation in *I* (from the viewpoint of the key!). The very next morning, as soon as she got up out of bed, she immediately found the lost key.

In order to constantly remember my status as a magician, it is helpful to *fully* retell the story in *I*, switching *all* appropriate nouns and pronouns into *"I"* and *"me."* Following is a story about how a certain family begins each morning.

I wake up in the morning and immediately climb up to warm myself next to me. Then I start fighting me, shouting, crying, cursing, and, losing my temper with me, smash my favorite me. Afterwards, I make a terrible fuss, not wanting to put me on, because I'm too tight, and I make it hard for me to breathe. I'm uncomfortably long, so I roll myself up. I can't wait for me to stop talking to me, and I can't stand it that I interrupt me. I yell wildly and slap me everywhere I can.

I become exasperated as I abuse and hit me. I go to my big me and knock myself against my concrete me; I drop me, putting a hole in me. I knock me against me, tear my new me apart, weeping bitterly, and beg that I take pity on me. I want to die; I hate me, and take me away from me.

Here is our question to you: How many different characters are described in this retelling?

Conclusion to the Theoretical Section

Everything in this book may be wrong.
Richard Bach—*Illusions*

The magician's techniques described in this book are just some of many possibilities for helping people unlock their creativity. Magic is not a dogma; it is a course of action. Express your creativity! *Develop your own techniques and personal world view!* The techniques are not the point. You simply must know that you are a magician, who, with sparkling eyes, joyfully participates in creation.

We often receive letters asking the same question: "Have I applied the technique correctly?"

In response, we suggest this world view: *Everything that I do, I do in the best possible way.*

This is a phrase from that Bible of magicians *Between Two Chairs* by Evgeny Kliuev. The book's heroes, Ruler of the Word and the Show Queen, declare to Peterpaul, who embodies the common world view:

RULES MAY BE MADE UP
IN THE MIDDLE OF THE GAME!

Magical Stories

I have so many problems that there is just no more time for me to perform any magic!

Statement by a seasoned magician

Favorite Stories

Battling Obesity

The art of soaring is a fairytale land for me: it helps me cope with all kinds of life situations in this complex world; it is a return to childhood when I was the center of the universe; it is positive psychotherapy; it is a way to heal myself and others; it is the ability to engage my "enemies," who soon afterwards often become close friends; and it is the art of watching and seeing, listening and hearing, feeling and perceiving. The art of soaring is not a withdrawal from reality, not just another shell to hide in where it is warm and dry, but rather it is movement forward, flying on the wings of imagination—I am the one who spins the wheel of life.

Like so many others, in seeking spiritual sustenance for my ravenous mind, I devoured a multitude of teachings in pursuit of truth, which kept slipping through my fingers right when it seemed that I had finally managed to seize it by the tail. I felt caught up in the rat race, constantly running in circles in search of the meaning of life. This frenzy could have continued with no end, if this silvery island, shining with the light of beneficence, hadn't appeared on my path, instilling in me love for myself and for everything—the art of soaring! My introduction to this system came about through a series of intriguing circumstances.

After giving birth to my son, I became extremely depressed by how drastically it had altered my outer appearance. I wished that mirrors everywhere would be shattered, and that people who had known me before the birth would view me only through the prism of love, and not so blatantly refer to my increased weight. Unfortunately, everyone could clearly see the changes which had occurred. In order to rid myself of "my eighth chin and third stomach," I started battling against my weight in earnest: I exhausted myself with calisthenics, wrapped myself in cellophane, ran three miles a day, massaged my face, did breathing exercises. At night I performed practices out on the balcony to recharge my subtle energies. But nothing improved.

Once, at a spiritual seminar, I saw a scrap of paper covered in writing with a strange word standing out: SHAMARON. That evening I found myself uttering this word over and over like in a counting rhyme, and writing it all over a notebook page. When I woke up the next morning, I started repeating it out loud again. Finally I stopped myself, concerned that I was obsessing on this meaningless word way too much, and for a while I forgot about it completely. Pulling myself together, I ate breakfast and set out for work.

I don't like walking to work because our roads are so muddy and slippery; no one ever cleans them. Therefore, as I walk along, I like to sing to myself or listen to a CD player. That morning, as I was leaving my apartment block, I started singing: "And I will pray for you before God that you may have a resplendent SHAMARON, SHAMARON..." I winced, chastened myself, glanced around, and, seeing that no one was paying attention, burst out laughing.

Arriving at work, I could hardly wait for my break, so that I could call the Director of our Holistic Center, Mikhail, to find out what this SHAMARON thing was all about. Mikhail told me that I was too late. Recently there had been a seminar, but personally he didn't really believe any of it. "A couple of magicians—pretty weird stuff. But the people who came seemed to really love it."

Once a teacher of transcendental meditation had given me a personal mantra which I didn't like at all. I tried to find out from him why he chose that particular combination of sounds, and whether it could be changed. The teacher told me that the mantra could not be changed, but if another word I liked better came to me, then I could repeat it instead of the mantra. I never did find the right combination of sounds, and in the end I abandoned the practice.

In order to discover the meaning of the word SHAMA-RON, I decided to use it like a mantra for meditation. Every evening, in spite of the sidelong glances of my housemates, I shut myself up in my room, turned off the light, closed my eyes, and repeated this mysterious word. One night it carried me off to… goodness knows where! Houses and trees spun around in the air, and a huge mirror rose up right in the middle of the street. I was standing next to it, combing my hair with a golden comb. A beautiful face and slender body were reflected in the mirror, and I thought: "Where's the double chin? And all those extra pounds?" I couldn't help but love *the one reflected in the mirror*—she was beautiful; she radiated light. It was enough just to be in her presence.

When I emerged from this meditation, I felt a little sad, yet tranquility and self-confidence had settled in my heart. Sometimes at work during my lunch break, I would sit back in my chair and utter this "magic" word, and the longed-for image of the beautiful woman would appear. After work I would run home, looking forward to seeing the one standing before the mirror. I tried to believe that we were one and the same.

Two months later, I was invited to yet another spiritual seminar. The women there kept remarking that somehow

I looked different. They complimented me, saying that the changes were not only in my outer appearance, but that I was radiating an inner tranquility; even people who had always ignored me in the past came up to me. It was astonishing, and I felt very happy.

Arriving home, I dashed to the mirror and noted with pleasure that my double chin had disappeared—I had lost over twenty pounds. "Hooray! Hooray!" I shouted out loud. I wanted to call Mikhail to find out when the next magician's seminar would be, but Mikhail was reluctant to give out his home phone number, so I only had his office number. I started repeating my secret word again. About an hour later, a woman from our club called, whom I had previously known only in passing. She happened to have Mikhail's telephone number. I immediately dialed the number and tearfully nagged him to organize another seminar on magic. He laughed and said that the seminar had already happened, and that he didn't plan to sponsor another one just for my sake.

After that I often closed my eyes and repeated over and over: "I am waiting for SHAMARON." My girlfriend laughed at me for this, saying that I was obsessing way too much over this strange word "that didn't even exist." One evening, my meditation was interrupted by a phone call from Mikhail, who announced excitedly: "You wanted a magician? Well, get ready; he'll be arriving very soon." I don't remember what I said, but I was completely overcome with joy, like once when I was given a teddy bear for Christmas.

I understand now that I was in a state of soaring. I pictured in my imagination what a magician might look like—an exceptional person with a hypnotic gaze, charismatic voice, and a peculiar appearance. All my thoughts were consumed by my upcoming meeting with a real, live magician.

What do you think? What should a magician look like? Perhaps, you too can visualize one in your imagination. Well, okay, I won't beat around the bush. I'll just say that I was utterly stunned by what I saw. Sitting in his chair, slowly rocking, was a slovenly man with disheveled hair in a checkered shirt with rolled-up sleeves and baggy, worn-out jeans. You couldn't even tell what color his eyes were behind his large, tinted, rectangular glasses. This portrait was finished off by an entrancing, openhearted smile, like the smile of the Cheshire Cat, which seemed to exist all by itself. I thought: "I've been waiting for this teacher for so long! Is he going to just sit there and smile, rocking back and forth in his chair for the entire seminar?"

Not looking at me, Oleg, the magician, grinned mischievously and uttered: "Throughout this seminar I will be continuously pulling your legs while rocking back and forth in this chair. Not everything that I tell you will be true. If you like, you can believe me; or if not, you don't have to. Whatever pleases you."

Even when speaking about serious matters, Oleg kept smiling, and it was impossible to tell what he really felt about what he was saying—everything seemed to have some kind of double meaning. Despite my frustrated hopes of meeting a powerful, charismatic personality, for some reason I didn't leave. I desperately wanted to find out how the seminar would end. With a generous helping of humor, Oleg explained magical theory, supported by real-life stories. Gradually everyone relaxed, and by the end of the day I had come to the realization that this was, indeed, my teacher!

On the second day, the people at the seminar were completely transformed—their eyes shone; they smiled joyfully at each other; they laughed at themselves and their "impossible" problems; and they danced. The gloomy, tight-lipped skeptics who had been glowering at Oleg the day before became happy and talkative. And you say that miracles don't happen? All this occurred because Oleg was in a state of soaring and able to transmit this to us, probably by renaming many of the participants. I still wonder what name he might have given me.

After the seminar my friends kept remarking that I had somehow grown much prettier; I had slimmed down, and my eyes seemed to shine brighter. I felt an unusual lightness in my movements, a kind of spiritual liberation, and, most importantly, I truly believed that I was a magician who could perform miracles. Naturally, I began to utilize magical techniques in all aspects of my life.

The Frog Princess

I can tell you one thing, Ronkhul: as long as a person remains alive, nothing is lost. There's always an exit out of any situation—in fact not just one, but several. Who are you to believe that you're the first human being in the entire universe to fall into a truly inextricable situation?!

Max Fry—*Nest of the Chimera*

For the past seven years I haven't had any luck at all with men. Three times I was married. Each time everything went according to the same script: I would meet a man I liked, but before long I was "carrying him on my shoulders," and in the end he was like a "suitcase without handles," whom I would drag awkwardly behind me. I have everything I need, and the men who came into my life would use me without the slightest twinge of conscience.

Most recently, I fell in love with Andrey, who, as I later learned, turned out to be married. He would come to see me only when there was a crisis in his family.

One day I was complaining about my life to a friend: "I've had it! What's the point of living? I don't care about anything anymore…"

"Well, I can help you out. Here are some notes about magic. You should take a look at them."

Reading through them, I realized immediately that this

91

was exactly what I needed. Seven pages dealt with the theory of renaming, and five others told real-life magical stories.

Studying them over very carefully, I filled up a bath with hot water and plopped down into it. I was determined to stay in that bathtub until I'd come up with an image and chosen a new name. I relaxed and closed my eyes. Time passed and still no image came. Soon I began feeling sorry for myself and burst into tears. I don't know how long this continued, but suddenly an image finally appeared: a green frog was sitting in a marsh with an arrow in its mouth.* So I took on the name: *"I am the one who catches the arrow."*

For several days I repeated it. Unexpectedly, things began to get better between me and Andrey, and we became close friends. Previously, I would cry whenever he called me to say that he couldn't meet that night, but now I felt completely calm. In the end he pretty much disappeared, but even that didn't bother me.

Before long, this change in my inner state began to be reflected in my two daughters as well. My older daughter was getting almost all A's in her grade book, but until then, being so wrapped up in my personal issues, I had not paid any attention to this. My daughters were both taking lessons in English. In the past, I would lose my temper when the girls couldn't learn a word, but now I appreciated how well they were able to read both Russian and English.

For an entire month, I was constantly reminding myself that *"I am the one who catches the arrow,"* and it gave me a deep

---

* In the famous Russian fairytale *The Frog Princess*, an old tsar orders his three sons to shoot their bows in any direction and marry whomever picks up their arrows. The youngest son's arrow is picked up by a frog, whom he marries. The Frog turns out to be an enchanted princess of amazing beauty and wit. [trans]

inner peace. I thought: "Who cares? All these men—it's no big deal!" As it turned out, it wasn't a guy I needed at all, but rather the support which I now found inside myself.

One evening I went to the spiritual dances, and a man came there named Mamedananda—one of the long-time dance leaders—who had just returned from a journey abroad. I had never seen him before. In the past, I had been extremely shy, especially around leaders, but seeing Mamedananda, whom everyone had been waiting for with great expectation, I repeated to myself: *"I am the one who catches the arrow."* For the first time in my life, I didn't feel awkward. I was relaxed and spoke with him easily and naturally. When I met him a second time, he took me by the hand, and since then we have never been apart. I had trouble remembering his strange name, so I just called him Quasimodo.

Before meeting him, I had always had the feeling that I should do something important with my life, but when I met Mamedananda, I realized that this was it.

After that another problem was resolved of its own accord. In the past, it had always bothered me that everyone else got to take vacations abroad, but I never got to go anywhere. Gradually, I came to understand that it doesn't make any difference where I am—more important is what's inside me.

An interesting transformation occurred in the image of the frog—the single slide had transformed into a moving picture showing it shedding its skin and transforming into a beautiful maiden, singing and dancing at a feast to the indescribable joy of the king. I became *"the one who sheds my skin."* This name well expressed my process of liberation from several severe psychological complexes.

When I first saw *The Art of Soaring*, I immediately knew from the cover that this book was for me. After reading the introduction, I became absolutely convinced of it—the authors spoke to me in a language I could understand! In the evenings, I would read the book aloud to my girls, who insisted that I never open it without them. I was always happy to find anything in common to share with my daughters. *The Art of Soaring* brought us together for many hours, thanks to the numerous quotations from children's literature and the tale about Feodor. After finishing the book, we practiced magical techniques together to realize our dreams.

The magical dances intrigued me. I thought that since I had mastered renaming on my own, then surely I should be able to learn the dances as well! One evening, when no one was home, I focused on this intention, and my body "by itself" began to move about in outlandish ways, accompanied by mantras which seemed to come out of nowhere. While performing these movements, I felt that at last I had found the perfect closure, and I bound it all together with the final mantra. Everything had worked out again! Hooray! Hooray! Hooray!!! The intention which I had expressed through that dance was realized effortlessly.

Through a series of amazing circumstances, I also got to travel to England. I didn't have an invitation, a visa, or any money, yet everything fell into place in just one week. It's interesting that I had heard about the festival in England and about magic on that very same day that my friend had taken me to the spiritual dances. There I learned that a Russian group was planning to go to England for the annual International Dance Camp, and I had a strong premonition that I would be going with them. In the notes that my girlfriend had given to me that night, I had read about the technique of "testing the waters," and I put it to use straight away. As I walked along the street, I thought: "If a man overtakes me, this means that I will travel to England, but if it's a woman— I won't even try."

Hearing the sound of heavy boots behind me, I rejoiced: "Thank God! A man!"

But it turned out to be a little girl.

"Holy moly! What's that supposed to mean?"

Right then two foreign luxury cars passed by, packed full of men.

"Everything is going to work out!" However, first there would be some small obstacle, easily overcome, but then more good than I could even imagine.

And so it happened. In order to resolve certain issues around my visa and money, instead of scheming how to get around them, I simply started *"catching the arrow."* The invitation arrived very quickly, followed by my English visa. I managed to sell my motorcycle to the first person who responded to my ad—I had been trying to sell it forever—for the exact amount I needed for the trip.

Mamedananda has many friends from all around the world. I had a wonderful time, and his friends were sincerely glad to see Mamedananda so happy. Everyone seemed to agree that we were perfect for each other. One kind Englishwoman said: "Your love will strengthen you, and you will be able to offer much to the people around you."

Changing Reflections

There is Shadow and there is Substance, and this is the root of all things. Of Substance, there is only Amber, the real city, upon the real Earth, which contains everything. Of Shadow, there is an infinitude of things. Every possibility exists somewhere as a Shadow of the real. Amber, by its very existence, has cast such in all directions... Shadow extends from Amber to Chaos, and all things are possible within it... If one is a prince or a princess of the blood, then one may walk, crossing through Shadows, forcing one's environment to change as one passes, until it is finally in precisely the shape one desires it, and there stop. The Shadow world is then one's own... to do with as one would.

Roger Zelazny—*Nine Princes in Amber*

Having attended innumerable esoteric and psychological seminars of every imaginable kind, I began healing people. I primarily used the Juna method of noncontact massage and managed to achieve astonishing results—I cured every single patient who came to me. I was especially proud of the times I healed cancer patients, most of whom suffered from thyroid cancer.

One day a woman came to see me, and discovering that we had a mutual friend, we started up a conversation. Having heard about my "achievements," she admonished me: "Why aren't you afraid of receiving such seriously ill patients at home? You've got a small child, haven't you? Don't you know that many bioenergetics practitioners treating cancer patients often become cancerous themselves? See, cancer is the result of severe karma which you can bring onto yourself."

Her impassioned words made a strong impression on me, and I quit my practice. Looking back, I now understand that, instead of feeling intimidated by her negative worldview, I should have simply laughed at its "inviolability" and remembered that I am a magician in charge of my own reality.

About three months later, I decided that I needed to see a chiropractor, so I went to a medical cooperative. There a young man, touching my neck, declared: "You must go to an endocrinologist right away to check out your thyroid gland!"

The endocrinologist sent me to the Oncology Department, where I was examined by a very famous oncologist who in no uncertain terms delivered a cruel verdict: "My dear, poor girl, I'm so sorry to tell you that you have only about two or three months to live. You must have an operation immediately."

I asked him: "But will the operation help?"

He could only answer: "I can't tell you if it will help or not, but it really doesn't matter; you don't have much longer to live in either case."

At home I fell into hysterics. I felt desperately sorry for myself. I was going to die at such a tender young age! Sobbing bitterly, I told everyone at work about my grief, and they all pitied me deeply. I was tortured by the thought that my mother would not be able to survive my death, and that my eight-year-old son from a previous marriage would be left alone (I'm now remarried). I discussed his future with my first husband, Dmitry, with whom I still had excellent relations, and he promised to take custody of my son in the event of my death. My mother discussed with Dmitry the legal technicalities of child custody.

I went to the Oncology Department at the hospital, up to the seventh floor where they perform neck operations. All around were patients with tubes stuck in their throats, and the constant sound of gurgling—like with professor Dowell's head*—was very depressing to me. The same movie kept rolling through my mind, showing me suffering with those same tubes in my throat, day after day slowly withering away, enduring unimaginable pain. The rooms were dirty, painted a dull gray, and I couldn't bear thinking about lying in one of those beds. I decided against the operation; I would wait for my end at home.

I was brought up in a religious family, and my grandmother had always taught me that a person should prepare for death both spiritually and materially. So I went to church, prayed, and confessed. Remembering that my grandmother had been buried in a blue brocade dress, I had one just like it custom made for myself. I would put it on in front of the mirror, cross my arms over my breast, and imagine how stunning I would look in the coffin, and how everyone around would pity me, so young and so beautiful. I even bought blue shoes, and someone gave me a pair of blue embroidered tights from England. I worried about how to arrange everything so that the elegant stitching would be visible.

I didn't want to be buried in a cemetery, since the movie in my imagination showed how, slowly but surely, the maggots would devour me and my beautiful blue dress. Instead, I imagined my body cremated in a bonfire in the forest—not scattering the ashes, but digging them into the earth and setting

---

* Reference to a well-known work of Russian science fiction, *Professor Dowell's Head* by Alexander Belyaev (1925). At his death, professor Dowell's head is separated from his body and maintained alive, connected by tubes to medical equipment. [trans]

a large boulder over them to serve as my gravestone. I had a letter notarized, which gave permission for my corpse to be burned anywhere (there was no crematorium in our city).

My close friends and family were also drawn into this game. Many tried to discourage me, unable to imagine how a corpse could be burned up completely. I had become the script writer, director, and starring actress in a grandiose, life-and-death drama.

What's more, I attended a seminar, in which they taught us to visualize our gravestone with an epitaph carved into it. I saw written on mine just one single word: "Person."

One day a colleague at work dropped a book by Roger Zelazny onto my desk—*The Chronicles of Amber*. He declared that this book should be required reading for every person on a spiritual path. I looked down at the book, trying to determine whether it was worth reading. It looked like a children's book, so I decided to leave it there at work.

When I arrived home that evening, I had to chuckle—my persistent friend had snuck *The Chronicles of Amber* into my handbag. My God! What a marvelous world the author portrayed! The enchanting adventures were so engrossing that I felt like bursting into tears when I turned the final page. It was so sad to part with the characters of the book. Over and over I shifted and changed the reflections of Amber at the center of creation, altering the very structure of my body. Instead of my former nightmarish pictures drawn all in the darkest colors, I found my way to new, wondrous reflections, translucent and bright. In short, this amazing book brought me into a natural state of soaring.

Three days after finishing the book, I happened onto a seminar of magicians, where I learned to incorporate humor into my process. Looking back at my death sentence, I chanted my new name: *"I am the one who changes reflections."*

After the seminar everyone noticed a dramatic change in me—my eyes radiated light; I was constantly laughing and joking; and it became increasingly easy for me to see into people.

A month passed, and I completely forgot that my time to die was fast approaching. One day my mother reminded me of this, and we decided that it wouldn't hurt to go for an examination. I again visited the Oncology Department, where I underwent numerous tests. They recommended that my thyroid gland be surgically punctured, which a famous professor would perform. It was terrifying to think about my throat being pierced. But the devil is not so terrible as he is painted—it was nearly painless.

Finally, I went for my final evaluation with the professor. He started yelling at me: "Why have you been needlessly wasting the valuable time of so many doctors? Why were you even referred to us? There's nothing wrong with you!"

I can't even remember how I made it home—my legs felt like noodles. I dug out my former diagnosis and called the professor. Hearing my voice, he slammed down the receiver. Nevertheless, I went to him with the original diagnosis, showing him the x-rays and doctor's prognosis. I even quoted the "death sentence" given to me by the venerable oncologist.

Examining them carefully, the professor uttered in amazement: "Strange things happen in this life; for some unknown reason all your ailments have simply disappeared."

Moving

Pronounce the word "Oviotganna" as often as you can—that's my advice to you. Repeat it out loud as you follow me through the forest, repeat it as you fall asleep, and also when we part—the more, the better. This is your opportunity to gain power quickly.

Max Fry—*Nest of the Chimera*

I had a small, 140 square foot room in a three-room communal apartment. Two other families also lived in that apartment: an old granny and grandpa, and a middle-aged couple with two children—the father was named Grisha. This family occupied a dirty, rundown, 175 square foot room with four beds, a table, and a large wardrobe dividing it into two sections. Each morning I would be startled awake by a piercing screech on the other side of the wall—my neighbors were moving their beds to clear out a passage. And in the evening, the sounds of moving furniture rang out again as the family got ready for bed.

Grisha was an alcoholic, sometimes drinking himself into such a delirium that the following day he could remember nothing about what had happened to him the night before. Sometimes, when he was in an especially bad mood, he would chase his family out onto the stairwell, reveling in his harsh threats and the crying of his children.

Grisha's children were very unhappy. The younger one, Antoshka, had a habit of stealing things, and the older,

101

16-year-old Tonya, suffered from epilepsy. Grisha was un-employed, so his wife, Sveta, had to support the entire family. Due to the harshness of her life, she had become completely hysterical, and her loud yelling was constantly heard com-ing out of their room. Sometimes the family tried to resist Grisha's aggression, and once the daughter even knocked him over the head with an empty bottle, drawing blood. Again Grisha drove his wife and children out of the apartment. The next morning he did not remember anything, later finding out what had happened from his wife. He was ashamed of his behavior, but whenever Grisha got drunk, his pent-up resent-ment would flare up, and he would start after Tonya.

Grisha was a tall, thin man with a gray, withered face. He usually wore a dirty, striped vest, like sailors wear, and torn pants. When sober, he was a jack-of-all-trades—he could fix a faucet, washing machine, even a television set.

One evening, Grisha drove his family out onto the stair-well again. At the time, I was giving my five-year-old son, Maxim, a bath. Grisha, enraged and cursing, tried to force his way into the bathroom, but the door was hooked closed. When I realized that there was nothing I could say to stop him, and that he would only just break off the hook, which would then have to be repaired, I opened the door for him. The brute pounced on me. I ran out of the bathroom, so as not to frighten Maxim. Sure enough, Grisha chased after me, and my son was able to finish his bath in peace. I raced out of the apartment and pounded on my neighbor's door. She let me in, and I summoned the police. When the policemen arrived, Grisha continued to rage, brandishing his fists, and in the end the officers had to use their billy clubs to subdue him. When they had taken the troublemaker away, Sveta pounced on me, shrieking uncannily: "How could you! Even as it is he can't get any work; now it'll be even worse for me and children!"

Incidentally, she quickly calmed down. The following day, her husband returned home, bruised and battered.

I finally decided to arrange for the sale of this accursed communal apartment which entailed finding suitable apartments for each family. There was no lack of people who wanted to buy our apartment, but the deal would always fall through. Perhaps one reason for this was my intense desire to sell it as quickly as possible. Every time someone came over to look at it, I would swoop down on them, trying to persuade them to buy it.

Having become acquainted with magical techniques at a seminar, I started renaming those who looked at the apartment—mainly by using imaginary pictures. I gave them names like: *"I am the one who plays baseball."* Results came quickly. Potential buyers stopped shying away from me; they called back and came for a second look, or a third.

After that I went to a gathering. There I met Beard* and asked him to help me with the apartment. First, he proposed that I find an object of power in the apartment, something that I had a good relationship with. The gas water heater immediately came to mind. Next, Beard suggested that I make an agreement to collaborate with it. Gazing inwardly, I pictured the water heater in my mind and began to describe out loud its indisputable merits.

"O, Gas Water Heater! The elegance and grace of the lines of your white-enamel body truly are worthy of an artist's brush. The secure, airtight hood of your chimney, like a knight's helmet, directs the combusted gasses towards freedom. Your admirable metal controls with spherical, ebonite knobs allow for the smooth regulation of your flame. The symphony of your steady hum possesses a rare depth and intensity. You are

* Beard and Papa are the authors' nicknames. [trans]

one of the primary centers of our small, communal universe; without you all would be cold and lifeless. It is my honorable duty to care for your welfare and normal vital functions. I promise to regularly clean you and ensure that your flame is lit only after you have been filled with water."

During this monologue, I completely forgot myself, trying to merge with the water heater. I could sense how pleased it was by my attention, which it had never felt throughout its entire life.

In the dim twilight of White Nights at the camp, you could still make out the crowns of mighty pine trees and the dark, still surface of the lake. The resinous, aromatic smoke rising from the juniper branches which blazed in the campfire only intensified the mystical mood around us. Beard was performing a dance. The bizarre movements of his body in the glow of the fire invoked feelings of forgotten ancient rituals. His final mantra left us spellbound: CHIKALAMPA. Beard "uploaded" this mantra into the gas water heater. Then he drew out of his windbreaker pocket a small, burgundy-colored stone, a garnet, whispered something to it, and handed it to me. A sharp point on the stone invigorated me, and I liked it immediately.

When I returned home after the gathering, Grisha had lessened his demands. Previously he had wanted a two-room apartment, but now he agreed to two rooms in a three-room apartment—yet still in a Stalin-era building in a prestigious neighborhood. Grisha and Sveta proved to be extremely picky. They looked at nearly fifteen different possibilities, and each time something wasn't quite right—the kitchen was too small, or the person sharing the apartment was horrible. Besides, my troublesome neighbors were convinced that I was trying to deceive them and had contrived some devious scheme to make out with a pile of money.

Sveta would sometimes go off into hysterics: "Well, I really could not care less! Maybe we'll just stay here, and spend the rest of our days glaring at each other between these walls. So what if it's worse for me. I'm not going anywhere!"

I placed my small stone on a narrow ledge above my table. I would often hold it in my hand, talk to it, and then carefully return it to its place. I also conversed with the gas water heater, repeating CHIKALAMPA, while renaming any potential buyers of the apartment. Suddenly the gas water heater broke down—a pipe had ruptured inside it, and water was spraying all over the place. This caused everyone in our communal apartment to become more amenable. I was glad for this, figuring that the water heater had adopted this tricky maneuver in order to make the transition easier for us. The granny and grandpa agreed to a one-room apartment in a remote district, and Grisha said that he "would go anywhere, just so it's done with as soon as possible." He repaired the water heater, winding asbestos cloth around the pipe, and warned me: "This will hold for maybe a week, so we should move out before then."

I called around to all of the real estate agencies and continuously danced CHIKALAMPA in front of the water heater, caressing it affectionately. Throughout that day buyers arrived in droves. Finally, I settled on a nice married couple. A handsome, well-built man, Arkady, and his plump, attentive wife, Glasha, tenderly cooing at each other, made such a favorable impression on me that I didn't even bother looking at their apartment for trade, taking them on their word.

At the same time, options were found which were acceptable to the remaining occupants of our communal apartment, and we quickly drew up the required paperwork. Grisha and his family, and the old couple as well, all got what they wanted, and I got a fantastic two-room apartment. The entire transaction cost me only five thousand dollars—an extremely modest sum for St. Petersburg. Moreover, the agency which closed the deal didn't take a commission, which would have cost me about three thousand dollars.

It took us a long time to move out of that communal apartment, especially Grisha, who, as it turned out, had a lot of possessions. For instance, there was a cupboard in his room packed full of cereal grains and bottles of sunflower oil which he had purchased with food coupons. I was continually renaming Arkady, who had bought our apartment. Without complaint, he patiently waited while we moved out. Arkady had hired some of my friends to renovate the apartment, and when it was done, he invited me to come over to have a look. I didn't even recognize it—spacious, light, comfortable, with leather-textured ceilings. Kittens were frolicking everywhere, and Glasha, gently rolling around the floor like a doughnut, treated my son Maxim to some tangerines. I felt a bit sorry for the old gas water heater which had played such a major role in the whole drama—they had replaced it with a new one.

The Building Cooperative

We either make ourselves miserable, or we make ourselves strong. The amount of work is the same.
Carlos Castaneda—*Journey to Ixtlan*

Three years ago my wife and I invested $18,000 in a build-
ing cooperative. They promised us that the building would
be finished in six months, and at that time we would receive a three-room apartment. Three months later, I visited
the building site and saw that nothing had started—there
wasn't even a foundation. At their office, they gave me various excuses—the project had been delayed because they
were unable to lay down a high-voltage cable, etc. Then
they offered us an apartment in another building, which
was expected to be completed within the same timeframe.
I agreed. However, nothing happened with that building
either—it just stood there half-finished without a worker
in sight.

Over time, they got to know my face very well in that office—I was on a first-name basis with the manager, Alexander Kondratievich. They would recognize my voice on the
telephone and immediately tell me that the manager was not
in. Then they offered me an apartment in yet another building
which would be finished in a year. A year passed. At the next
investor's meeting, the director of the cooperative promised
that in three months one of the buildings would finally be

done, and we would receive our apartments. As you may have guessed, this promise fell through as well.

Alexander Kondratievich periodically "fed" me various promises—evidently, just to stall time. Finally, my wife and I gave up all hope for an apartment, or even to get our money back; for all intents and purposes we had "buried" it. We told ourselves: "Well, what's the point now of beating ourselves up over $18,000?"

In the summer of 1997, we went to a Summer Solstice Festival in Karelia north of St. Petersburg. On the last day of the gathering, our friend Valya informed us: "There are some interesting magicians here; let's go over and see them."

I'm kind of a stick-in-the-mud type—it's often hard to convince me to go out—but Valya somehow managed to get me there. At the seminar, we laughed non-stop for three hours straight, and then the leaders began renaming everyone. Valya dragged me up to them and I received the name: *"The one who curls hedgehog quills."* I liked it.

Late that night, we left the festival in our old car, so overloaded that a guitar had to be balanced precariously on top of the heads of the three people sitting in the backseat. Just before we reached the city, there was a police check point at a traffic signal. While watching for potholes in the road, I accidently ran the red light. The traffic cop stopped us, and everyone in the car started desperately renaming themselves. I became *"the one who wags his billy club like a tail"* (this name has helped me many times since).

"Why did you run that red light?" the officer scolded me.

"Well, actually, I was watching out for potholes."

"Step into the booth and sign the register."

I registered,* and he let me go without a fine.

---

* This took place at the end of the Chechen war, when they were registering all cars entering and leaving the city.

The next day I remembered my comical image. Grabbing an empty plastic container, I started pounding out a rhythm on it while dancing and singing: *"I am the one who curls hedgehog quills."*

Right then the telephone rang. It was Alexander Kondratievich: "Hello. I'm happy to say that we can now refund your money. How much would you like?"

Over the past three years, the cost of housing had significantly risen, so I considered asking for $25,000-$27,000, but my wife started poking me in the side and whispering $30,000.

"Thirty thousand," I answered.

"How about twenty-nine?"

"No, thirty; twenty-nine is not enough."

"OK, make it thirty. But I can only give you eighteen thousand now; the rest will come later."

"When can I get it?"

"I'll call you."

This time Alexander Kondratievich kept his word and over the next two months made payments to me totaling $30,000.

The Iron

"They say a book is the best gift."
"No," Emma Ivanovna retorted tearfully. "The best gift is an iron."

Evgeny Kliuev—Book of Ghosts

At work I had been assigned the task of submitting a delinquent financial report of a certain company, which promised to be an extremely complex project. This was my first independent job—at that point I only had a few bookkeeping classes under my belt. What's more, one of my co-workers had been telling me horrible stories about an evil comptroller at the Employment Fund who never, ever accepted delinquent reports.

During a group meditation at a seminar on magic, I saw an interesting image: an iron appeared on a white background with its cord stretching upwards, and a plump, smartly-dressed woman was holding the plug in her hand. I decided to name myself *"the one who walks the iron."*

I liked this name very much, and after receiving group support for it at our next meeting, I decided to charge it with even greater power. I generally strike people as a person without a lot of serious issues. Therefore, I thought maybe they would brush me off, thinking that I was just seeking attention. Of course, I could have renamed the whole group, but at that time I wasn't brave enough to even consider that. A magician's "audacity" is directly proportional to his experience.

So I thought up this ingenious ploy—to bring an iron to the seminar and walk it around as in my vision. I went over to see a friend who had an iron similar to the one which I had seen in my meditation. He didn't call an ambulance to take me away; he wasn't even all that surprised at my request. I guess that's what friends are for—to love and understand us.

We performed many lively exercises at that seminar. I was walking around the hall, followed by the creaking iron which I was pulling behind me. Some of the exercises were done with eyes closed, and people would giggle whenever they bumped into me.

The next day I set out to submit the report, bringing the iron with me. It was accepted with flying colors by the Medical Insurance Fund. The comptroller listlessly asked why it was late, checked only one other document, and affixed the required seal. Next was the Employment Fund, the one which my co-worker had been scaring me with. As I was walking up to the building, I started *"walking the iron."* The comptroller fully lived up to her reputation. She was obviously in rapture at the opportunity to freeze our bank account, and she refused to stamp the return. The desire flashed through my mind to whack her over the head with the iron, but that would hardly have helped the situation.

I went outside, fished out the iron, and took it for a walk in the freshly-fallen snow. This definitely made us happier, and we continued merrily on our way. In order to check how good my chances were for a successful completion of the affair, I decided to bum a cigarette from the next passerby. I set the conditions beforehand that if the person didn't give me one, then I'll do nothing; if he did give me one, but it's a cheap brand, then I'll summon up all my strength to finish the job; but if he gives me a good cigarette, then I can relax and just follow the flow. I was treated to a "Marlboro"!!!

I was getting ready to go to the Social Insurance Fund, when I suddenly noticed another support signal—two dogs humping in the street. Renaming myself as *"the one who is humping on the pavement,"* I cheerfully set out for my goal. At the Social Insurance Fund, they wanted to send me away, but, perhaps realizing that I had a heavy object in my handbag, they finally accepted the report. At all my remaining stops, everything went like butter.

I had four out of five seals in hand and on the next day set off for the Tax Office. I had left the iron at home, but my shoulders still felt its invisible presence. In my mind I was still walking the "iron beast." And guess what? The tax inspector didn't ask to see a single seal, and the financial report was duly registered!

To my amazed co-workers I explained that I had managed to do all this thanks to the iron. This has now become the all-time favorite joke in our company, especially during tax reporting periods. I didn't forget my helper, the iron, although I did return it to my friend. I still take it for walks in my mind, and sometimes even go visit it. My renaming has helped me a lot in my work—I'm on time wherever I go, I encounter only accommodating auditors, and lines are always short, or there are no lines at all.

Soon after all this happened, they started playing a song I really liked on my favorite radio station. Later on I saw the video. In it, someone was walking an iron!!! But the one doing it wasn't shown on the screen. I have no doubt that it was me. So here was one more confirmation of the power of intention—the internal movie made real in life.*

---

* This story produced a very powerful impression on the authors of this book and has been highly inspirational to many participants at their seminars. In particular, the theoretical section "Transfiguration" was written under the influence of this story.

The Labyrinth

"What am I thinking about? Well, of course, about Eternity. What else is there to think about? Immortality might be nice... For the most part, I don't think about anything and wait for an alternate Eternity, an alternate Infinitude to descend from above, ripping this world to pieces. But whatever the outcome—time will no longer exist... You might even say that this is what I'm invoking."

The stranger suddenly completely lost it. He jumped up from his chair and started running around the table, waving his arms so wildly that it seemed his hunchback slipped down a little.

He started sniveling: "You should be sent to prison, straight to prison! My dear fellow, how can you say that? Are you joking? Time will no longer exist! And what about beer? What about babes? Are you that indifferent to the pleasures of life? To prison with you, to prison!"

This astonished Cherepov. "You can't frighten the higher powers with prison..."

"There are no higher powers if you don't invoke them... But you're confusing people and nature. If only there were an international law to prosecute you under, you vile Plato!

Yuri Mamleev—*Rambling Time*

After August 17th our family fell into deep financial difficulty.* Our daughter Svetlana was working in a bank, but it
collapsed, and she lost her job. The business I worked for was
also suffering severe losses. Things weren't going so well for
my husband, Konstantin, either. As bad luck would have it, at
that time he got into an accident with an expensive foreign
car. Our savings in the bank had disappeared with the financial crisis, so there was no money to repair the car. Konstantin
started drinking "out of grief."

This is when I began attending meetings of a local group
of magicians, and after only three weeks our family started
getting back on our feet.

Arriving home one evening from a meeting, I suggested
to Konstantin that he try kneading some clay with his hands,
relaxing and not thinking about anything in particular. The
result was a pathetic, shapeless blob, in which you could barely make out a kind of head and two legs. On the whole the
figure was rather pitiful, and Konstantin exclaimed: "Am I
really that bad off?" He was so struck by this creation that,
without any renaming at all, he managed to stop drinking and
no longer snuck out to the garage "to relax."

At our next magician's meeting we created a collective
mantra for attracting money: TUFUNDENDA. I decided to
pass it on to Konstantin. For a long time he resisted, refusing
to repeat it, but nevertheless kept the slip of paper with the
mantra written on it. Soon afterwards, I managed to borrow
some money, and the car was quickly repaired, costing only
half of what we had expected. Then, a few days before the New
Year, Konstantin received a nice sum of money, and we were
able to repay most of our debts. I suspect that my husband

---

* On August 17, 1998, the ruble collapsed, causing severe hardship for
the Russian people. [trans]

continues repeating this mantra even to this day. And while previously he was annoyed whenever I went to a magician's seminar, now he is glad that I go to them.

When Svetlana was little, Lewis Carroll's *Alice in Wonderland* was her favorite book. After reading *The Art of Soaring*, my daughter exclaimed: "This is exactly what I need!" I had arranged some work for her, which she didn't like at all. She finally decided to quit, although I tried to talk her out of it: "Wait a little. Times are tough now. First find another job, and then you can quit."

Svetlana was unperturbed: "Don't worry, mama. After all, I've read the book!"

She set herself up at a realty agency. No sooner had she begun work than she closed two transactions, astounding even her more experienced colleagues. As it turns out, Svetlana had diligently applied the techniques of testing the waters and paying attention to signs.

Our major problems were satisfactorily resolved, but there remained one very longstanding issue—I was terrified of audiences. I work in a managerial position, and as part of my duties I often have to give speeches in public. On the night before a talk, I would fall into utter despair. Before the speech, my hands would get cold, and my voice would stutter and shake, even though I was always superbly prepared and knew exactly what I had to say. What's most amazing is that in the process of giving the speech the terror would gradually disappear, and I would calmly and confidently finish my presentation.

At the seminar, one of the participants renamed me with the help of a dance, during which he depicted an arbor. The dancer imparted the mantra KANDUK LAPARTEN, adding that a little hedgehog was running around the arbor.

I immediately recalled that we have an arbor at our summer-house in the exact same shape, and that a little hedgehog did indeed live there.

When I arrived home, I went up to the window and looked out onto the street. The sun was shining in a blue, cloudless sky, reflecting brightly on the countless crystals of freshly-fallen snow. I started repeating the mantra, dancing around the room, and then, still standing, fell into deep meditation. My body was vibrating intensely. Free verse burst out of me; there was no time to make it rhyme, or even to remember it.

At that point I saw clearly what life is really all about. It's like we are all haphazardly wandering around a dark labyrinth, searching for happiness in all the usual ways—work, money, family... At first, we search for ourselves in one thing, then in another, but we always reach a dead end, because there is no exit out of the labyrinth. In the end, there is nothing left to do but go back to our starting point. We begin to realize that this life is all illusions, and that the real issue is to be freed of this labyrinth of conventional values.

In my vision I emerged from the labyrinth and found my-self on the bank of a narrow, swiftly-flowing river with whirl-pools swirling across its surface. Not far away, I could hear a thundering waterfall. Inwardly I knew that I had to somehow reach the other shore, so I dove into the river and fearlessly swam across. As I emerged from the water on the other side, I saw in front of me a tall mountain with snow glistening on its peak. A multitude of paths ascended it. I knew immediately that I must climb to the top of this peak, which symbolized victory over death. I could have died in the dark labyrinth, on the way to the mountain, or on some high plateau, but at the top of the mountain peak there would be no death.

After this meditation, I went out and came across the book *The Wizard of the Emerald City*. I had been wanting to reread this book for a long time and, arriving home, "swallowed" it all in one gulp. I felt an affinity with the Lion (that is my astrological sign), considering myself a coward inside, but in real life—fearless. I decided to perform the ritual recommended by the Great Gudvin—to drink down a potion of courage.

I brewed up some wild herb tea in a thermos, placed it on a chair in the center of the room, and performed the Lion's dance around it. At first he felt frightened, but in the end, actually becoming the lion, *I filled the jungle with my resounding roar*, experiencing myself as the true king of beasts. I received a mantra with which I magnetized the tea, and then I slowly sipped the potion of courage out of a saucer.

You could say that, after the meditation, the dance, and the tea, I went into a state of soaring. Before I had been living in stress, always expecting misfortune to strike at any moment, but now I feel an unusual lightness; everything seems to just turn out well on its own. There's probably no need to add that my fear of giving speeches in public completely disappeared.

How Magicians "Corrupted" a Psychotherapist

"Rules can be made up in the middle of the game!" objected the Show Queen. "And as for the melon, put it on your noggin... I've played for long enough. You are a terrific partner. The very cheerfulness of it all will be the death of me... You should never seize on what is obvious to everyone else. What's the thrill of repeating what everyone already knows. Whatever anyone else can figure out isn't nearly so interesting as what you alone can figure out.

Evgeny Kliuev—*Between Two Chairs*

The Amazing Toy Dumbbell

I've worked as a psychotherapist since 1994, over the years practicing neuro-linguistic programming, holodynamics, psychogenetics, Ericksonian hypnosis, different kinds of psycho-analysis, and psychodrama.* A year ago, I experienced a crisis in my work—I became disenchanted with many of the techniques I'd depended on for so long. Because of my confused state, my pool of clients started drying up. A difficult task lay

---

* This story is narrated by a young woman. [trans]

before me: how to rediscover myself in psychotherapy and increase my flow of clients.

My introduction to practical magic was a true revelation. The system is simple and coherent, and its basic premises correspond to my personal conception of the world. After devouring *The Art of Soaring*, I started using magical methods, personally and in my work with clients.

One day, after a long-standing client, Tamara, had finished telling me her "tale of woe," I asked her: "What's happening in your life that's good?"

"I like having tea with my neighbor."

"And how do you have tea with your neighbor? In small bits? Or do you put her whole right in your cup?"

Tamara pictured how she might have tea with her neighbor whole in her cup, and burst out laughing: "Actually, my neighbor looks like a teacup herself—she's round in every way."

I told her to repeat: *"I am the one who drinks tea with my neighbor in a teacup."*

This was the first time ever in my practice that a client left my office fully satisfied after only twenty minutes. Later on, Tamara told me that her issues had been quickly resolved—in particular, her relationship with her son had appreciatively improved.

One day a friend telephoned me: "Some magicians are dropping by today. Do you want to come over?"

I went to meet them, hoping that they could help me find a way forward.

Two men—one bearded and the other in heavy glasses—listened to my story. They mysteriously exchanged looks and in one voice proclaimed: "Now you will be transfigured into something new." I couldn't remember reading about this technique in the book, so I was intrigued. For a while we sat in silence. I thought that the magicians had probably entered into some kind of deep cognitive state, and I awaited their holistic solution.

Right then my friend's dog—a Rottweiler named Alba— dashed into the room, clutching in its teeth a toy rubber dumbbell, which it was shrilly squeaking.

The charlatans livened up: "Definitely a support signal!"

The man who wore glasses instantly went down onto his hands and knees in front of the dog, saying: "I want to chew on it, too!" And he cautiously nibbled the edge of the dumb-bell.

Intrigued by the antics of the silly man, the dog cocked its head to the side and pulled the toy back slightly towards itself. The man wouldn't quit until Alba finally gave up the dumbbell, which the magician began gnawing furiously. The dog watched all this bug-eyed.

Then the bearded man turned to me: "You, too, get on your hands and knees and take the dumbbell away from that mutt."

I had been expecting pretty much anything but not such utter insanity. I had thought that maybe they would delve deeply into my past and give me some kind of referential name to work with. I felt embarrassed; the entire situation seemed so completely idiotic.

"I am a down-to-earth adult woman," I thought, "and they want me to get down on my hands and knees and gnaw on that slobbery toy dumbbell covered in hair?! What do they take me for?"

At that point the bearded man also jumped down on all fours and started squeaking the toy. Looking down at these two normal-looking men excitedly crawling around the floor, I realized that they had nothing else to offer me. Feeling like a complete fool, I got down on all fours. The dumbbell had hardly touched my lips when I was stunned—I wanted to gnaw on it, too. The conscious part of me protested: "What are you doing? This is ridiculous!" But my body responded pleasurably; it liked gnawing on that piece of rubber.

Returning home, I washed off my new object of power, put it in my handbag, and started regularly nibbling at it. I began to feel an inner, spiritual balance and decided to fulfill a long-term dream—to learn to drive a car. The instructor turned out to be most unpleasant—he was constantly yelling at me and making obscene proposals. Once during driver education class, the teacher announced that he was going to divide us into two groups, so that each group would have its own instructor. My last name was on the second half of the list, which meant that I would wind up with that obnoxious man again. There was nothing to lose. In front of everyone I pulled the dumbbell out of my handbag and started chewing it. The teacher looked at me intently and drew the line under my name, assigning me to the other instructor. That's when I truly became convinced of the effectiveness of nonsensical ritual.

Unexpectedly, I was invited to attend a training seminar in "Symbolic Drama," which I had been trying to get into for two years. Afterwards, all the techniques that I'd previously worked with came together into an elegant system which reflected my inner worldview. At that same time, I received an offer to appear on local television to give a series of lectures for parents whose children were about to enter the first grade. Ever since that very first broadcast, the telephone in my office has never stopped ringing—I now have all the clients I could ever want.

Circus of the Absurd

When visiting Common Sense... you do not wear canary-yellow shorts, striped leggings, or a bathing suit... you do not carry a parrot on your shoulder or a toad in your hand... you do not lie sprawled on the floor or hang by the chandelier... you do not keep silent, nor shout "Everyone, watch out!" nor do you bark or quack... you do not eat balloons... When leaving Common Sense, you do not walk out on your hands nor be thrown out head over heels... You do not take away from there a wardrobe or fried chicken hidden under your clothes.

Evgeny Kliuev—*Between Two Chairs*

Over the next year I attended several intensive training seminars in magic. The use of humorous techniques always yielded instantaneous results. What I especially liked was that you didn't have to dig deep into the past or future; you could change everything in any given moment. The controlled silliness—like gnawing on the dumbbell—was very appealing to me. I started regularly performing magic and giving out absurd recommendations.

Once an acquaintance came to me with a delicate request. Ivan wanted me to introduce him to my close girlfriend whom he had seen at a party. I explained that my friend wasn't attracted to him, but the ever irrepressible "don Juan" kept insisting that I become his matchmaker. He called me every day, reproaching me for being unfair, and finally came to me for a consultation. While we were talking, I noticed that Alba, who was standing nearby, started sniffing at Ivan's briefcase. I renamed myself as *"the one who sniffs the attaché case."* Ivan still wouldn't give up, so finally I promised to think it over. On my way home on the bus, I started sniffing at my handbag, which was shaped somewhat like a briefcase. The man sitting next to me looked up in consternation. Opening the handbag, I sniffed its contents, causing my neighbor to sniff the air apprehensively while moving farther and farther away from me.

At eleven o'clock that night Ivan called me. "I'm sorry I've been such a bother. I now realize that I should really sort things out on my own."

One of my clients complained to me that, after her bathroom had been remodeled, glazed tiles started coming loose. Zoya was extremely anxious that the contractor would refuse to fix the problem. Right then Alba started barking excitedly, wagging her tail, so I recommended that Zoya do the same. The next day, completely dumbfounded, she told me that the construction foreman had called and asked her if anything needed to be repaired.

My ten-year-old daughter's leg was bothering her. Sashka had participated in a hilarious magician's seminar with me and asked for some sort of outlandish recommendation. I suggested that she sprinkle buckwheat groats out onto the table and peck at them with her nose.

Sashka, barely managing to hobble up to the kitchen table, poured out the buckwheat and asked: "Is it OK if I nibble them?"

"Nibble away."

She carefully chewed the buckwheat kernels and got so carried away that after just fifteen minutes she was hopping about the kitchen like a chicken.

I was astounded. "How's your leg?"

"What about my leg?"

Since then buckwheat has become an all-purpose elixir for Sashka.

Whenever my daughter acts up, I instantly start renaming on the wing. Usually within five minutes she's back in a great mood. Children love to play magical games.

Recently something interesting happened. Sashka was whining: "Mom, I want some ice cream, but I don't want to go get it. Mom, I want to draw, but I lost my markers."

I looked around the room, renaming myself out loud: *"I am the nesting doll; I am the green pencil; I am the little monkey; I am the number five on a piece of paper; I am the tights under the chair; I am the little dinosaur on the bridge."* Unexpectedly, like a highly-skilled illusionist, I pulled out from a hidden corner the markers which Sashka had lost over two months ago. Overjoyed by my discovery, she rushed out to buy some ice cream.

All you loving mothers out there! Instead of scolding and chastising your child, I recommend, as a professional psychotherapist, a remarkable method—renaming on the wing. Rename yourself out loud with whatever happens to catch your eye. I especially love composing whimsical names: *"I am the panda bear which palms; I am the pen which cases on the table; I am the notebook with inkafied squares."* It's best to find names which are funny, that awaken joy in you. Then everyone starts having a good time, and your child's mood will instantly improve.*

---

* The authors believe that renaming on the wing can also be very effective with a drunk husband or a quarrelsome mother-in-law.

The Remote

There are three Buddhist methods for watching television… First you watch television with the sound turned off—for about half an hour each day, your favorite program… Then you start watching television with the sound turned on but the screen turned off. And finally, you watch with the television turned off completely. This, really, is the main technique, but the first two are preliminary steps. You watch all the news programs, but you don't turn on the television. It is very important that while doing this you sit with a straight spine, and it is also good to fold your hands over your stomach—the right hand first, covered by the left. This is for men; for women it's the other way around. Don't be distracted even for a second. If you watch television in this way for ten years straight, even for just an hour each day, you will understand the nature of television—and of everything else as well.

Victor Pelevin—*Generation "P"*

A client whom I had helped the previous year returned to me for a consultation. Tatiana told me that she had to take her final exams at the Institute before their scheduled time, but the Assistant Dean, Felix Markovich, refused to grant authorization. This was my seventh consultation that day, and I was tired of delving deep into the personal histories of patients, of saying over and over again phrases like: "Your relationship with the Assistant Dean replicates your relationship with your husband, your stepfather, your father," etc.

I pictured Tatiana sitting in front of the TV, continually changing channels with the remote. I spoke to her with the voice of a prophet: "After you arrive home, at exactly 12:00 o'clock, sit down in front of the TV and use the remote to switch around between programs. Watch each one for five minutes. While doing this, repeat to yourself: '*I am the one who changes channels.*' Afterwards, when you go to the Institute, take the remote with you, again repeating the phrase and pressing the buttons."

Two days later, Tatiana told me this amazing story:

As you suggested, I switched channels while sitting in front of the TV for half an hour, watching the first six programs I found. All my anxieties vanished. I felt light and at ease; even watching the commercials was enjoyable.

The next morning, thinking about the remote, I decided: "This is stupid. Why bother taking it with me?" But as I was leaving my apartment I caught sight of the remote in the hallway lying, as if on purpose, in a highly visible place. Who put it there? I have absolutely no idea. I was hurrying to make the train, so quickly shoving the remote into my pocket, I dashed out. The last train before a long break in service had already left, and the buses weren't running either. I was at a loss of what to do—it takes an hour and a half to get to Moscow from our town.

Standing there perplexed in front of the station, I started pressing the buttons of the remote. Suddenly, a car screeched to a halt right in front of me. A friend's face was peering out the window. "Hey! I'm going to Moscow. Do you want a lift?" I climbed into the car, and thinking about my impending meeting with Felix Markovich, I furiously pressed the remote buttons. On the way we got stuck in a traffic jam, but again I "changed the channel." A foreign car in front of us suddenly turned off onto a side street, opening up an escape route, and we broke free of the pack. By the end of the ride, my fingers ached from so much pressing on the buttons.

Throwing my coat and handbag to my girlfriend who was waiting for me in the corridor, I entered the Assistant Dean's office. Felix fixed his eyes on me: "What do you need from me?"

I suddenly realized that in my rush I had left my "magic wand" in my handbag and leaped for the door, uttering: "Oops! First I have to go get my remote!"

A few seconds later, I was again sitting in front of Felix and, holding my hand in my purse, furtively pressed the buttons. He stated flatly that he was very busy, and he quickly signed the required document.

My girlfriend was astounded by my success: "Nothing's working out for me. What can I do?"

"Wait a second. Here, take this remote; just keep pressing the buttons."

She was glowing when she walked out of the Dean's office.

Tatiana later came to the conclusion that the remote could work for anyone in any situation. But she wondered: "Can I buy a second remote to carry along in my purse? After all, we need one at home for the television."

"Go ahead and get a second one," I answered her, "but it should definitely have a red on/off button."

I regularly lead various psychological training seminars, and I told this story at one of them. My students decided together: "Tomorrow we're all going to buy remotes!"

In the past, whenever a client came to me, I would use techniques of classical psychotherapy. But now, when I listen to a client, I immediately picture that person in some kind of comical way. I can hardly contain my smile, wanting to offer some absurd recommendation, which, in fact, I frequently do.

So this is how magicians "corrupted" a psychotherapist.

Tales of a Freckle-faced Redhead

My Dream Job

> You are never given a wish without also being given
> the power to make it true. You may have to work for it,
> however.
>
> Richard Bach—*Illusions*

I am a designer of women's clothing by profession. I used to
accept private orders and sew clothes for clients, but in the
depths of my heart I had always hoped to find work in my
specialty. In an attempt to move in this direction, I opened
up my own shop, since—thank goodness—I had plenty of
clients at the time. But not long afterwards my dreams were
shattered by harsh reality—I was overwhelmed by a mass of
boring logistics. Most of my clients lived in Moscow, and
I was constantly running around the city, spending a large
portion of my income traveling and buying supplies. We had
trouble keeping up with the rent, and over the next year my
shop changed locations several times.

That summer was a complete disaster for us—people had
left town for resorts and their summerhouses, and finally I
was forced to close the shop for good. I was up to my ears
in debt both to my clients and to my workers, and so decided to find work in Moscow. Armed with the phonebook,
I called around to various firms and agencies and sent out
my resume. All that month I felt like a fish out of water,
flopping desperately against the ice. One rejection followed

another. In the end, I was so worn out that I wept for an entire week.

I started accepting occasional orders again to try to pay off my debts. The recent financial crisis had incited my creditors to start demanding payment from me, and wanting to settle accounts with them quickly, I was working around the clock. I managed to pay off a portion of my debts, but then a new disaster struck.

One of my elderly clients had ordered a coat to be made from her own fabric and mink dating back to the 1980's. I came up with an exquisite way to trim it out, purchasing the leather and other materials I would need with my own money. When the woman arrived for her next fitting, she stated plainly that she did not like it, and in fact no longer wanted the work done at all. I proposed either to return her money, or to redo the coat. In response, my client huffily demanded an enormous amount of money for her old fabric and long since discolored mink. I didn't have such a sum, and she went ballistic, demanding that I return her money immediately. She wouldn't give an inch. She kept calling me several times a week, even threatening to send "intermediaries"—that is, street hoodlums—to clear up the matter. I was scared stiff, my fingers were all thumbs, and for whole days on end I would lie on the couch vacantly staring up at the ceiling.

It was in this state that I happened accidently on a seminar of magicians. I came up with this name for myself: *"I am the one who slips off her sweater with a single, easy movement."* I liked this name very much and, arriving home, playfully practiced gracefully slipping off my coat and sweater. Three days later, I received a call from a newly established firm, and they proposed that I come in to discuss a position as a clothing designer. The office was just a fifteen minute walk from my home.

I was elated and started frantically preparing myself for the interview. But treacherous thoughts kept creeping into my mind—maybe they wouldn't give me the job after all. On the way to the office, I unfastened my jacket, slightly lowering it over my shoulders, and all concerns vanished. I opened the door to the office of the Director General like I was entering my own home. Unzipping my jacket, I plopped down onto the deep leather armchair, which puffed out a burst of air, and casually said: "Hi! So what kind of proposal do you have for me?"

My greeting was so forward that the director blushed deeply, dropping his pen. As he crawled under his desk to retrieve it, he overcame his confusion and, emerging, started talking about my future work. The following day they suggested that I apply for a passport, so I could travel to an exhibition in Turkey.

This is how I came into the job I had been dreaming of for fifteen years. The pushy woman with the mink vanished without a trace, and over time I was able to pay back all my outstanding debts.

The Canary Islands

However easy magik is, you can't let it look easy. You need a few hand props, a line of patter... Garkin's hut, where I had first been introduced to magik, had been full of candles, vials of strange powders, dusty books ... now there was a magician's lair! Of course, I had since discovered most of what he had was unnecessary for the actual working of magik itself.

Robert Asprin—*Myth Conceptions*

Engrossed in my work, I didn't notice that I had caught a mild cold. I forgot about my magic, and over time the disease worsened. My ears became infected. For two weeks, I languished in bed with a high temperature and horrible pain in my ears. Then the doctor heard a rattling in my lungs and diagnosed bronchitis.

Later that day a friend called me: "Some magicians are coming to give a seminar. Are you going?"

"I'm really sick right now and don't know if it's worth dragging myself over there."

"You should come, so we can rename you."

The following Saturday at the seminar, they gave me a new name: *"the freckle-faced redhead with pigtails relaxing in the Canary Islands with her little trowel and bucket."* Resolving to embody this name immediately, during the lunch break I rushed down to "Children's World," bought a toy trowel and bucket, filled it with millet, and for the rest of that day I continually stirred the "sand." My friend drew large freckles on my face with eyeliner pencil and attached on either side of my head "pigtails" made from a bright-red Christmas wreath. I even decided that after the seminar I would dye my hair red.

That evening we all gathered for a sauna, and I thought about how the air in a sauna is like temperatures in the Canary Islands. So my son and I constructed a sign. On a rope stretched between two palm trees, long, striped Nike swim trunks were hung out to dry. Above them in huge lettering were the words: "THE CANARY ISLANDS." My little daughter, thinking that the swim trunks were a tent, drew in between the legs a freckle-faced redhead and three feet sticking out of the tent.

I was surprised: "Masha, why are there three legs?"

"C'mon, mommy, you wouldn't be alone in the Canary Islands, would you? There's someone with you."

In the steamy sauna I lay sprawled on the upper bench with the Canary Island sign hung above me, playing happily with my little trowel and bucket to the friendly laughter and joking of everyone around me.

The next day I felt much better, and by Monday was completely healed. On Thursday, I went in for a routine medical exam with some of my woman co-workers. The first thing I noticed as I stepped into the clinic was a large mural depicting palm trees and sandy beaches.

The physician who examined us exclaimed: "What could possibly be wrong with such beauties as these! But why are there marks of cupping glasses on your back? You had bronchitis? That's odd. Your lungs are completely clear now."

Comical Rituals

There have been many times throughout my life that I have depended on pickles. Through joy and despair, the pickle has been an eternal companion to me; it helps me find myself, make decisions.

Sometimes in a moment of indecision, I only have to bite into a pickle—and instantly my vision becomes clear. If there are worn-out thoughts in my head, if anxiety and darkness trouble my heart, a pickle will always extract them, soothe them, take them away.

Yuri Koval—*The Lightest Boat in the World*

While preparing for my business trip to Turkey, I submitted the required documents for a passport which I needed by January 22. They told me at the Department of Visas and Registrations that the passport would not be ready until January 24.

At that time I was attending a seminar on magic, where we were learning to create comical rituals. I asked Sashka, the ten-year-old daughter of a fellow magician,* what I should do to get my passport on time.

She recommended this: "Cut up three apples into quarters. Then, over the next two days, nibble a little off each slice while dancing the Lambada."

* Cf. the story "How Magicians 'Corrupted' a Psychotherapist."

I performed this ritual very carefully, and my children helped out by also nibbling at the apple slices. On January 21st I received a call from the Department of Visas and Registrations: "Why haven't you picked up your passport? It's been ready now for quite a while."

After this experience, I started handing out "silly" advice right and left. My 14-year-old son, Maxim, had long dreamed of getting a computer, but I never had the money to buy him one. When yet again he asked me for 200 rubles to buy some computer part, I finally ran out of patience, advising him to munch dill seeds from a can of marinated tomatoes for three days in a row.

My son looked at me like I had finally lost it completely, but all the same prudently saved out some seeds. After he had chewed on them for two days, my sister unexpectedly gave him a computer, monitor, and printer. She was convinced that the computer was broken and had planned on giving it to a technical school, where a computer science instructor was going to try to repair it.

The computer turned out to be functioning perfectly well. Afterwards, I told Max that, had he chewed the seeds through that final day, he probably would have gotten a brand-new computer.

My friend Tonya was driving me nuts, describing to me in minute detail all her problems at work. Finally I got tired of it and suggested that she buy a "puzzle magazine" (one with crosswords) and pound it with a wooden mallet in a red washbasin .

Tonya brushed me off: "Oh, come on! That's crazy!"

A week later, she came running back to me: "Sveta, I need your help right away."

"Did you pound the magazine?"

"No, I don't have time for that now. I bought new furnishings for our entryway, but in order to install them, the front door has to be re-hung. My husband hasn't consented to any of this yet. In fact, he doesn't even know that the furniture is arriving tomorrow. I'm desperate. What should I do?"

"Get some deodorant, spray it all over the floor, and wash it."

"I'll even sacrifice my favorite brand—*Rexona*—for this."

Three days later, Tonya called: "The deodorant worked great! My husband noticed a pleasant fragrance in the apartment, and he himself offered to help re-hang the door. I'm off to get a puzzle newspaper right now to start pounding it!"

In February, I was working twelve hours a day without any increase in my salary. So I thought up this ritual: I would place several "magic stones" of different colors into the left pocket of my coat and run my fingers through them. I bought some color-glazed raisins, sprinkled a handful into my pocket, and fingered these magic stones on my way to work.

Three days later my boss, Oleg Borisovich, called me into his office: "Don't worry, starting tomorrow I'm going to double your salary."

The director had large, blue eyes, and secretly I used to call him "my little kewpie doll." Once Oleg Borisovich fell ill and didn't come to work on Monday. This troubled me greatly.

"Why should such a cool guy get sick?"

I created an imaginary movie, which depicted the baby kewpie doll lying in a stroller with his rattles, sucking on a pacifier. Before falling asleep, I played through this movie yet again, adding several tantalizing details.

On Tuesday, Borisovich appeared back at the office. I gave him this advice: "You're like a kewpie doll to me, so in order to recover completely, you should repeat: '*I am a kewpie doll, sucking on a pacifier.*' And I promise that I'll give you a real kewpie doll for your birthday. I even know that last night at 10:30 your fever broke."

"Yeah, you're right; it went from 102 to normal, and without any medicine at all."

"That's because I pictured you as a kewpie doll."

"You know, I figured that some kind of 'supernatural' powers were involved."

Olga's Achievements

So Juicy!

Well, I refused to introduce myself, and that is only because I don't know—really, I just don't know!—who am I... My name is either Oy or Luke. Is this good enough for you? To tell the truth, it doesn't suit me! I would prefer something like Zeus, if some name is needed.

Evgeny Kliuev—*Between Two Chairs*

I was in high spirits as I was returning home from a magician's class and spontaneously started renaming on the wing. The people on the subway looked depressed, worried, worn out by their day's work. So I searched for something pleasant in them, conjuring up various names in the process: *"I am the one who carefully ties his bootlaces," "I am the buckle shining on the sandal," "I am the one who sews on pearl buttons," "I am the eye glasses perched high on a nose," "I am the synthetic diamond earring bobbling on an ear."*

Throwing out names right and left, radiating joy, and smiling at everyone, I felt as if I were creating a new reality all around me.

Stepping out onto the street from the subway station, I realized that the trolley I was supposed to take had just left—there was hardly anyone at the stop. During the day, the trolley runs at 25 minute intervals, but late in the evening they are spaced much further apart.

Right at that moment a van rolled past me, and my attention was caught by an advertisement for bottled juice on its side—a big-eared mouse and a huge sign which read: "J7—SO JUICY!" My renaming was complete: *"I am the one who is SO JUICY!"* Glowing with satisfaction, I started repeating my new name. In order to allow a trolley to materialize, I turned my back to the direction that it would come from. A couple minutes later I could hear the familiar clanking of wheels knocking against the rails.

Now whenever I'm walking from the subway to the trolley, all I have to do is say: *"I am the one who is SO JUICY,"* and in exactly two minutes the trolley, as if by the flick of a magic wand, rolls up to my stop. It's amazing! But it takes about two minutes to walk from the subway platform to the trolley stop, so if I think *"I'M SO JUICY!"* while still at the station, then the jangling trolley car will take off right in front of my nose. So to get there on time, I have to enter the magical state in the underground crosswalk where it exits the subway station.

Flying on wings of success, I have been gradually altering my ordinary world view with every step. One day I had to cut up several onions for a pizza. In the past, this process would be a complete disaster for me. No sooner would I peel off the skin than tears would start pouring down my cheeks, and I would have to rush to the bathroom to rinse out my eyes. Even after rinsing them thoroughly, for half the next day I would walk around with red, inflamed eyes.

To deal with this, I pictured in my imagination a harlequin playing soccer in a tall cap and long, white gown with a lacy collar, red buttons, and sleeves hanging down to his ankles. His garb was definitely not well-suited for this popular sport, so to keep himself from falling, he bounced around alongside the ball. I imagined myself as *"the harlequin who plays soccer on a large green field,"* and as I cut up all those onions, not a single tear was shed.

After that, I "played soccer" another five or so times, and now I can slice up onions with complete calm, not even thinking about the harlequin.

A Zebra Riding a Carriage

"So you've not been performing any magic here?"
Khekhelf asked suspiciously.

"Well, as far as I can tell—no." I thought it over,
and then added truthfully: "But it's really hard to say
if something happens because you've been performing magic, or if everything is just working out on its
own."

Max Fry—*Nest of the Chimera*

At a magical seminar, people were given the opportunity to
step into the middle of the circle to talk about their personal
issues. Then the group would rename them. I spoke about
how I lost my job in the financial crisis. Out of all the offered
names, I composed this rather complicated one: *"I am a zebra
riding in a carriage, spurring it on with a fire poker."* The seminar leaders gave us the task of painting posters to depict our
new names so that at the next meeting we could organize a
triumphant parade.

I was visiting my son and his wife at that time, so that
evening I sat down with my four-year-old granddaughter to
paint the poster. She was such a cutie pie with her big blue
eyes and blonde ringlets, like the girl "Alenka" on the candy
bar wrapper. However, despite her angelic appearance, she
could also be extremely stubborn. It was especially difficult to
get our little beauty to eat.

140

There was nothing we could say, no punishment we could threaten her with to persuade her. Out of spite Mashka might refuse to eat anything for two or three days, only drinking water. At times I would completely lose it when my granddaughter would pick at her sandwich for an entire hour—walking around with it, climbing up onto the sofa, and acting out in every possible way. She wouldn't eat anything, spitting her food out or stuffing it into her mouth until she gagged.

That evening, when Mashka and I sat down to paint the zebra riding the carriage, I pictured a carriage with large wheels, gold monograms on its sides, and curtained windows like you see in historical films. I could see how it rocked lightly on its springs. When the zebra leaped up onto the carriage, the springs shuddered. There were no horses, so it thrashed the rear "bumper" of the carriage with a fire poker knotted to its tail, and the wagon rushed along at full speed.

As I was painting the poster, I couldn't help but feel that I myself was galloping over the rough ground in this wagon. Mashka helped me out—she painted in the poker. When the poster was almost done, she opened up a little book by Samuil Marshak, *Kids in a Cage*, to the exact page where a zebra is depicted galloping on two legs, its tail curved off jauntily to one side. Mashka then recited the verse:

> Striped horses,
> African horses,
> Let's play hide-and-seek
> In a meadow by a creek.

No sooner had we finished painting the poster than my granddaughter asked for something to eat for the first time in her entire life.

"Mama, let's eat something."

Shaken to the depths of her soul, her mother answered: "What would you like, dear?"

"Oh, anything, a cheese sandwich maybe."

After painting that poster, Mashka changed dramatically. Now she eats on her own, never raising any kind of fuss; in fact, she likes to eat just about anything.

Now about my work. I had formerly worked for a company which offered financial savings plans. After August 17, for all intents and purposes I lost my job—people simply stopped investing their money, trusting neither the banks nor the insurance companies. Wherever I went, I'd hear the same thing: "Are you out of your mind? What are you telling me? How can you offer savings plans, when no one has any idea what's going to happen next in our country?"

After attending a seminar in magic, miracles started occurring in my life, and I realized that I could find a way out of my crisis. I didn't have to wait long for results from renaming myself as *a zebra riding in a carriage*. Mashka and I made the poster on Saturday, and on Monday a girlfriend called me: "I just got a job offer from a promising start-up company. You should come over. They've got some real job proposals."

After visiting the firm "Russian Nugget" to find out more about its main lines of work, I was very satisfied. It is a national company engaged in multilevel marketing. And I like the product line offered by the firm—high quality Russian products with a promising future.

For instance, the company offers a unique biocorrector and spark plugs unlike any in the world, even better than the well-known "Bosch" brand. Another unique product in their line is a fuel additive which boosts octane levels fivefold, significantly increasing engine horsepower, increasing gas mileage by five to six percent, and lessening CO and CH emissions.*

Products are developed on the basis of torsion fields—information structures which are more subtle than atomic structures. Gasoline treated by torsion fields can be purified to the point that it will combust completely.**

All these inventions were conceived by one man—Alexander Fedorovich Panov, a student of Porfiry Ivanov. An inventor for over twenty years, Panov has been trying to develop a market for his products since 1990, and has just recently found a sponsor. According to experts familiar with his inventions, if he had chosen to market his designs in the West, he would have long since become a billionaire.

Realizing the bright prospects opening up for "Russian Nugget," I gladly joined their team. Panov—an extraordinarily gifted and creative man—made a deep impression on me. Once he explored the possibility of purifying certain liquids using torsion fields. He poured ordinary triple-strength *eau de cologne* into a bottle coated with butoxide resin mixed with metal shavings permeated by a torsion field. When I sniffed the contents of the bottle two weeks later, I felt that I would give anything for this fragrance.***

I started studying the technologies invented by Panov and helped market the products created from them. This brings me happiness and pays me well. Finally, I found the work I had been dreaming about for many, many years.

* Olga is solely responsible for the claims of this advertising information.

** In the opinion of the authors, an "all-powerful" torsion field is a clear example of introducing a new object into the common worldview (cf. "World View").

*** A beautifully formed, "persuasive" worldview is a great strength for a person with a rich imagination.

Visit to the Dentist

Understanding is the reward of fools.
Luke Rhinehart—*Transformation*

In closing, I will narrate another amazing magical story. I went to the dentist for a new crown, and he told me that a live tooth needed to be ground down . I was in a hurry to get to a meeting of our local group of magicians, so there was no time for a shot of Novocaine. I would have had to wait at least fifteen minutes for my mouth to become numb, and I was already late for the meeting.

Since childhood I have been dreadfully afraid of pain; I simply cannot bear it! Even the slightest pain would affect me terribly, and sometimes I would pass out. In the subway I often fainted from the slightest discomfort. People would have to carry me out of the subway car and call the nurse. I have always requested shots at the dentist's to avoid pain. Otherwise, I would lash out unable to restrain myself, struggling desperately to break free. Even though I understood the need for drilling, I couldn't control myself.

My dentist's name is Victor. He is a nice young man with a small mustache and crew cut and is very thorough in his work. He did a crown for me once and, knowing my extreme sensitivity to pain, warned me that this time would be painful without Novocaine. I would just have to bear it. Immediately, I started panicking. No sooner had the doctor touched the drill to my tooth than I jerked my body up sharply. I don't know how Victor managed to avoid stabbing me in the cheek with his drill.

Evidently, there was such terror in my eyes that the doctor asked sympathetically: "How are you doing? Are you afraid?"

"Uh-huh," I mumbled through my open mouth.

"It's nothing; don't be afraid. Everything will be just fine."

At that moment I remembered that I'm a magician. Victor started grinding the tooth, and in my fright I started repeating to myself: *"I am the one who looks at the patient with a drill in my hand."* I could smell the tooth burning yet couldn't feel a thing.

But my terror remained, and I thought: "It's sure to start hurting again any moment!" I looked around and noticed a wicker basket of artificial flowers with beautiful round leaves hanging off the tiled wall. I became *"an exquisite wicker basket with a garland of flowers."*

When Victor started grinding the tooth from a third direction, I was again transformed. Directly over my head hung a Chizhevsky ceiling lamp (an air ionizer which operates on the principle of glow discharge).

I named myself *"the Chizhevsky ceiling lamp whose needles watch the patient."* I didn't feel any pain at all. After finishing his work, the doctor, completely baffled, asked me: "Olga, what was up with you? Wasn't it painful?"

"No."

"How can that be possible? That was a living tooth, and you're so sensitive to pain."

"I transfigured myself."

"What? How?"

"*'I am the one in a white coat holding a drill.'* For instance, if you don't want a traffic cop to give you a ticket, transform yourself into the beautiful badge on his chest. It sometimes helps."

We laughed together, but Victor still looked bewildered. It seemed that he'd just decided that I was completely bonkers. I tried to explain: "You ground down my tooth three times. First I transfigured myself into you, then into the basket on the wall, and finally into the lamp. Can a lamp's teeth feel pain?"

"Um, no."

"Or a basket's?"

"No."

"That's why mine didn't hurt either. I was, after all, *'a basket with a garland of flowers.'*"

His office was large, and, hearing our conversation, the other doctors also burst out laughing. You could see what was written all over their faces: "That woman has definitely lost her mind!" I left the office to laughter all around me.

A Shy Woman with Many Talents

Mask of Emptiness

A person is free only when he is being silly engaged in delightful and unpredictable foolishness—like this, for example...

Ayid Alexandrovich took out a bottle of imported cognac from his briefcase; evidently, it had been a gift. He took two glasses from the table, filled them to the brim, and then walking up to the window, he slowly—with, as they say, deep feeling—poured the rest out... "This is for all of you," he shouted down, "to stimulate all your delusions of grandeur."

Evgeny Kliuev—*Book of Ghosts*

I am the department head in one of our security agencies. Once, at the end of a particularly intense work day, I decided to relax a bit and just do something silly. I remembered a mask I had recently brought to work. A friend, Galya, had made it for me. I've always felt that conceptions of "emptiness" and the "unknown" perfectly sum up the essence of this illusory world we live in. So I asked Galya to create a "mask of emptiness." I really liked what she produced—the blue-and-white papier-mâché mask expressed absolutely no emotion or thought of any kind, while at the same time expressing everything.

I put on the mask and stepped out of my office into the room where my subordinates were working. There were five of them, and each was busy with her own affairs—hunched over papers or staring at the computer screen—and they didn't even notice my sudden appearance. I stood there for about five minutes. At last Svetka, always on the ball, looked up, and the others soon followed her example.

My office is separated from my co-workers' room by a partition, which I was standing behind. Since I am short, they could see only the unusual mask set on top of the wall. I had expected a strong reaction—frightened outcries, laughter, or expressions of bewilderment. But instead everyone simply stared at me smiling calmly.

"Who's that?" someone asked.

And Svetka answered confidently: "Who else could it be but our Elena Sergeevna?"

I stepped out from behind the partition. Everyone took turns trying on the mask and looking in the mirror. It put us all in a happy mood, and we sat down together for tea.

Two days later I decided to wear the mask again but to walk around our building this time. I figured no one would be all that surprised. Once after a magician's festival, I had shown up at work outlandishly dressed. I was wearing a long, dark-blue skirt printed with huge yellow daisies, my jeans underneath, a bright-red blouse with tropical fruits sewn all over the front, and numerous colorful buttons on the back. My costume was completed by my favorite Indian mask. I'm awfully fond of sliding down banisters, so I climbed up to the fourth floor and intrepidly rode down the banister in this festive garb.

As I walked around the building in my new mask, someone sarcastically remarked that this is a serious institution, and if someone has mental problems, they shouldn't be working here. Another noted to me privately that other people aren't so liberated and most likely were even envious of me.

Generally, the men reacted very graciously—they were glad to be surprised.

At that point, I decided to wear my mask of emptiness into the office of our Division Manager. I was not trying to get any special favors, nor was I afraid of being reprimanded, or even fired. I was absolutely certain that nothing bad would happen—after all, a magician is a magician. I was mostly interested in seeing how Nikolay Andreevich, the top manager of our powerful security agency, would react.

To properly assess the true audacity of my behavior, you should know something about Nikolay Andreevich. This stern man, whom I had never even seen smile, was a true professional; he seemed to see right through people. Everyone was afraid of him. Whenever I heard his imposing voice over the phone, my knees would shake and a chill would run down my spine. I felt he might scold me like a naughty little girl. To be fair, I should add that he is a decent person who does not put down his subordinates as directors of other security agencies often do, and so he is generally held in high esteem.

That afternoon when I came in, his secretary was preparing coffee for Nikolay Andreevich. I let her go home, telling her that I would bring the coffee in myself. I heated up the water and put a teaspoon of Nescafé into a cup, adding a little Riga Black Balsam* which I always kept for such special occasions. Then, donning my mask, I glided into his office carrying the aromatic drink on a tray. I moved very carefully along his long table so as not to spill any coffee.

Nikolay Andreevich's face alternated between horror, dismay, astonishment, and indignation. He clutched at the arms of his chair as he slowly sank into it. It seemed that he was shrinking, as if deflating. Finally, drawing on a lifetime

* A traditional Latvian herbal liqueur. [trans]

of experience of pulling himself together under any circumstances, he regained his composure and gradually "inflated" back to normal size.

I expected that Nikolay Andreevich's voice would shake, or that he would burst into angry shouting, but he spoke in a clear, concise voice: "My most esteemed Elena Sergeevna, I've always known that you are unpredictable and stand out. As a rule, such people do not last long here, but you are a pleasant exception. I consider you a most valuable worker. We are currently discussing employee raises, and I've decided to raise your salary to the level of my deputies."

After this we discussed current events for a while, and the entire time I kept my mask on.

The next day I met Nikolay Andreevich in the corridor and saw a smile cross his face for the first time ever. After that, I completely lost all fear of my boss although everyone else still quakes on hearing his name.

My silly prank ended up bringing me a few perks. I can now leave work whenever I want without authorization, return late from lunch, or not come to work at all. Previously, I had to sit in the front row during morning meetings, and God help me if I was five minutes late. Now I come to work an hour later than everyone else, after the meeting is finished. Nikolay Andreevich calls to tell me when he'll be out of the office, and so on. No one understands why the director is so kind to me.

At Work

"Listen, who is the teacher here—you or me?" the
host started shouting.
"That has yet to be determined."
Voshche the Immortal apologized for his oversight
and stated:
"I am the teacher, not you. You must pay attention to
my words."

Evgeny Kliuev—*Between Two Chairs*

Once we had a manager in our office who was a true petty ty-
rant. Each morning Evgeny Georgievich would derive great
satisfaction from yelling angrily at the entire staff. This would
spoil everyone's mood for the rest of the day but seemed to
make the boss happy.

At a magician's seminar Georgievich was renamed as *"the
one who chases fluff around the room."* Each morning after that,
when I arrived at the boss's office for his daily thrashing, I
would affirm his "fluffy" name in my mind. This caused him
to forget what he was talking about and his sentences would
trail off. Georgievich would sit there nervously picking at his
nails, growing angry, and our daily briefing would be over.
Everyone started noticing his unusual behavior, and not
knowing why we were smirking at him, he finally called off
our morning meetings altogether. You can imagine how we
deeply drew in a collective breath of relief!

151

When I finally revealed to my colleagues the reason for the change, they decided that I should try this technique on yet another, even higher-ranking manager. Every day after our lunch break, Stepan Matveevich loved to walk between offices "hunting" for latecomers. If he found an empty chair somewhere, he would impatiently "lie in wait" for his victim who, relaxed after lunch and a cigarette, had simply lost track of the time, or was held up somewhere. Matveevich was terrible in his anger: "You're suspended! Fired! I'll teach you a lesson!" After barking ferociously like this for ten minutes or so, he would set off for the next office.

In order to refine my technique of imaginative renaming, I decided to apply it to Matveevich. I imagined Koshchey* sitting on the pavement next to a trunk filled with wooden toys and blocks. After momentarily considering what to do next, the Immortal One began moving the toys and blocks from one side of the trunk to the other. Dissatisfied with the results of his rearrangement, Koshchey started all over. So Matveevich was renamed as *Koshchey who moves the toys in the trunk while sitting on the pavement.* In my office I gathered together the co-workers I trusted, and we pronounced this new name aloud several times.

And what happened? A month passed, then another—the director wasn't anywhere to be found.

"Do you think he got sick? Maybe he's on vacation." My colleagues were curious. "Where is that old pike? Look, the carp are already nodding off."**

* An immortal evil spirit, character of Russian folk tales, often portrayed as spending his time counting his treasures in his chests. According to some sources, Koshchey had once been a kind wizard, but his image was gradually corrupted over time. [trans]

** Refers to a Russian proverb which states that it is the pike's purpose to make sure that the carp do not rest. [trans]

His all-knowing secretary reported: "He's at work but doesn't have any free time. Every week they keep bringing new furniture to Stepan Matveevich's office. Just when he manages to get it all arranged, they start unloading new cabinets. What a hassle! First getting them unloaded, then putting everything in place, and finally arranging for the next delivery, which means moving the 'old' furniture somewhere else."

As she was explaining this to us, Matveevich suddenly appeared.

"Oh, well. So much for our time away from him. Here we go again!" I thought.

But the director said warmly: "My dear friends, why are you still sitting in those old, worn-out chairs of yours? Go in my office right now and choose new ones."

This is how we got beautiful, new chairs with carved backs.

It was then Evgeny Georgievich's turn (the one who had chased fluff around the room). He blamed me for preventing him from properly managing the department, since I was the unspoken leader of the staff, and no one took him all that seriously. He had retaliated with various repressive measures against me. So I thought up a new fantastic image for him: *"I am the one who whitetops the elephant."* On that very day, a friend called and offered me a management position in his department at a good salary. I transferred to this new work and am now in charge of most of the staff. And so ends this epic tale of my relations with petty managers.

As it turned out, my new place of work didn't have modern office equipment. I turned to senior management. In answer, they told me that, while I'd worked there for only a few days, other departments had been waiting for computers for years. At that moment a friend called to invite me out to dinner.

I figured that this was a support signal and became *"the one who eats dinner in a restaurant."* A month later, all the necessary office equipment was installed in our department.

We also needed office supplies. I called the first advertisement I saw in the newspaper and, after inquiring about prices, discreetly asked the director if he would be willing to work out an arrangement with our organization. He answered that we could discuss the matter later. In the end, we managed to reach a compromise to settle our accounts through cross-cancellation of debts. In the same way we were able to get furniture and various expensive yet necessary smaller items. The managers of other departments are now asking me to share my secret. How did I possibly manage to do all this?

I try to resolve these issues like equations in a textbook, rather than get angry at myself and those around me. You just have to find that positive spark, and your internal magician will whisper softly to you: "Good going! Take off your sunglasses and appreciate how brightly this crystalline world sparkles!"

April 27th

From time to time it's fun to test our certainties, pretend that they're lies.

Richard Bach—*Running from Safety*

I was greatly anticipating the coming seminar in playful magic. When at last the long awaited day arrived, it began like any other: my husband, Dima, and I ate breakfast together, and he left for work. But then less than five minutes later he returned. He looked bewildered, and a ridiculous smile was plastered on his face.

"Did you forget something?" I asked.

He replied gravely: "Our car has been stolen."

I was astounded by my reaction to this dreadful news. Instead of hysterics and grief, a clear plan immediately came to me—where to call, who to write—but I completely forgot about being a magician. I just felt frustrated. I had been waiting for this seminar for such a long time, and because our Audi had been stolen, I no longer cared about any of it. Finally, I did decide to go to the seminar, although my friends advised me not to.

One friend said straight out: "How could you do all that silliness after losing your car? In fact, why do you take that garbage into your head at all?"

I figured it was unlikely that the Audi would be returned that day, but it was definitely possible to improve my mood, and that would help me find the car.

On the first day of the seminar, I felt generally out of sorts, but on the second day I realized that knowing I'm a magician gives me great power. I had told only one friend and the seminar leader about the car. The leader gave me this perplexing formula: *"I am the one who cruncheshires the burbulephant."* After repeating this funny name several times, I calmed down.

That evening Dima asked: "So you went to the seminar, but will it help us in any way to find the Audi?"

"Of course it will; we'll find it in twenty-seven."

When I arrived at work that Monday, my co-workers asked: "Have you found your car yet?"

"No."

"Then why do you look so happy?"

"Because a car is really just a car, but I was at an amazing seminar!"

Several times more I *cruncheshired the burbulephant*, and completely forgot about our loss.

On April 27th I came home from work, but Dima, who usually arrives before me, wasn't there. In fact, he didn't show up until 11 o'clock that night. Again a silly smile was plastered on his face, just like on the day the car was stolen. I immediately knew that something had happened.

"Do you know where I was?" Dima asked right away. "I went to identify our car! They found our Audi!"

A Samara Fairytale

Enchanted Verses

My wife and I were running our own company in a city center office which we rented from a man named Gregory. He had leased a large space and subdivided it into smaller offices. When the term of his lease expired, Gregory was having trouble getting it extended. For about a month and a half he promised that we could move into a neighboring building, but just before New Year's the deal fell through. We found ourselves in a difficult situation—we had to find suitable accommodations in the city center in just a few days!

Previously, I had been a physics teacher and had a student named Anton. He was a smart and enterprising young man, who now had his own business out of an office rented from Gregory. When Gregory announced that he had lost his lease, Anton was extremely distraught. He came to me, looking rather bedraggled—he wasn't wearing a tie, his coat was unbuttoned, his short hair mussed up—but his eyes were shining brightly. Anton casually announced that he would take care of everything—the whole world was at his feet. Tomorrow he would reach an agreement with the owner of the building which Gregory had hoped to lease for us. At that moment I chose a name for myself: *"I am that fellow who musses up the ground."* Anton was the *fellow* with *mussed-up* hair, but *ground* came out of nowhere.

About a year ago, I had begun writing verses. While attending a seminar in practical magic, I thought that, if soaring formulas were made into poetry, then their power would be greatly amplified by the rhythm, rhyme, and meter.

I decided to express my new name in verse. This inspired me, and filled with joy I quickly penned the following lines:

Past the city of Elets
A train is speeding, homeward bound,
In it sits *a clever fellow,*
The one who musses up the ground.

Broad-shouldered, svelte, a real stud,
Quick-witted, with the girls renowned,
In fact, that *clever fellow's me,*
The one who musses up the ground.

The train is rumbling through a tunnel—
Stars fade away, the night wears down.
How good it is that *I'm that fellow,*
The one who musses up the ground.

A stunning woman wrapped in furs
Feels my glance and turns around.
I'm that dashing, short-haired *fellow,*
The one who musses up the ground.

The following day Anton and I went to the landlord and immediately came to an agreement with him over the rent. I liked the premises very much—they were larger and lighter than our former ones and had been recently renovated...

Magician friends started asking me to compose verses from their own formulas for soaring. I've noticed that my intention begins to manifest the moment I start composing poetry. My wife asked me to put this image to verse: *"I am the flea which plays with ether and speaks Latin.*" Her intention was to attract more participants to the next magician's seminar. This is how it was expressed as poetry:

> To be seen from far away,
> I'm covering myself in kefir,
> *Speaking prophesies in Latin,*
> *I'm that flea which plays with ether.*
>
> Boldly knocking back a shot
> Of sake blended with fruit kefir,
> *Speaking prophesies in Latin,*
> *I'm that flea which plays with ether.*

The result exceeded all expectations—so many people came that there were not enough chairs for everyone. The room we had rented in the Community Center turned out to be too small, so we had to move to a larger one.*

---

* Renaming in verse, initiated by the author of this story, has become very popular in the world of merry magicians.

The Frolicking Umbrella

> If you will practice being fictional for a while, you will
> understand that fictional characters are sometimes more
> real than people with bodies and heartbeats.
>
> Richard Bach—*Illusions*

Since receiving training in practical magic, I am always using
the technique called renaming on the wing. Even my mother
stopped complaining about her ailments, although she has
had several mini-strokes, breast cancer, and other severe
health issues. At home I'm always repeating various strange
names, often also offering them to my husband, Leonid, but
he just waves them off.

Big problems were brewing at Leonid's work. His small
company was never officially registered because it had been
affiliated with a larger one. However, when the mother company was liquidated, Leonid's was suddenly a nonentity, and
the landlord was threatening to evict them from the premises. For two months Leonid "sat on boxes" in the process of
moving; over time all work ground to a halt.

One day Leonid arrived home from work completely worn
out—he looked like a ghost. I fed him, sat him down in his
armchair, and said: "C'mon, let's play together. You love playing with our dog and our kids."

Right then the final scene of the film *Umbrella Coup* with
Pierre Richard was on TV. Everyone was laughing, and I

uttered automatically: *"I am the umbrella which frolics in the swimming pool."*

Leonid started: "An umbrella? I like that. What's the umbrella doing?"

"It's frolicking. You should become a frolicking umbrella at work."

"Okay, but what if I forget?"

"I'll call and remind you."

On the first day, I telephoned him several times: "Hello, Umbrella?"

"Yeah, right, I'm still frolicking here."

"Just don't forget!"

My son also liked this name and asked: "Have you been talking to Umbrella?"

Once Leonid began *frolicking in the swimming pool* in earnest, he managed to get the new company registered in only two days. But in the meantime the company had lost its offices. I started explaining to him exactly how he should frolic: "Imagine that you are an open umbrella floating smoothly along and spinning like a top."

My husband liked this new image a lot and started imagining the spinning umbrella. Soon afterwards Leonid found new accommodations for the company, even better than the previous ones and located near our home. Furthermore, in the process he had met a local official who offered him a fifty percent discount on rent if Leonid would lead a computer study group for schoolchildren two hours a week. Leonid gladly agreed—he loves messing around with kids.

About that same time, I decided to buy some new winter boots. In order to achieve my goal, I too began *frolicking with the umbrella.* The following day, Gennady called my husband at work and suggested that he trade in his car for a new one. We had an old Zhiguli Model 4, and Gennady was offering a

1994 Volvo. Leonid was unenthusiastic, even when Gennady told him that as a favor he would sell him the Volvo at the same price he had got it for in Minsk plus gas to transport it to our city. An hour later Gennady appeared in person at Leonid's office—there was nothing to do but go look at the Volvo. That was it. Leonid could hardly tear himself away from his new toy, and the price was only *twenty-seven* thousand rubles.

We traded in our old car and got to keep the difference— two thousand five hundred rubles. With that money, during the New Year's clearance sales, I bought some fabulous English leather boots, which previously I hadn't even looked at, since they had been so highly priced.

A friend, seeing me in the Volvo, later asked: "Where did you get the money to buy that car?"

"Actually, we never even held it in our hands."

"C'mon, you're making that up. Volvos don't just fall from heaven."

"Actually, for us they do."

Our New Apartment

My husband, Vadim, works at a factory. His wage is ridiculously low, and lately he's been paid weeks late. The only reason he doesn't quit is because he is in line for a new, subsidized apartment which the factory had been building since 1990. Over time, though, construction had slowed to a complete halt, and no one knew whether the apartments would ever be completed.

Around that same time, I found myself at a seminar in magic, where I was renamed: *"the secretary bird who reflects sunbeams off a watch on its leg."* I started regularly wearing a watch around my leg, and in sunny weather would even try to reflect sunbeams off it.

Less than two weeks later, the Factory Work Committee summoned Vadim to tell him that it was time for him to collect the necessary documents to register our new apartment—we could move in! It was an epic task to gather together the paperwork needed. In the Registration Office, we had to certify that we did not own any real estate in the city. All adult members of the family had to be present, so the three of us—my husband, son, and I—arrived together. Several tellers were open, but each had a long line in front of them. We each queued up at different windows. Twelve minutes later, and the lines hadn't budged.

Suddenly I remembered that I'm a magician and thought: "Why are you just standing here? Do something!" In one of the windows I caught sight of a toy Santa Claus hanging

from a desk lamp (it was December 28) and started repeating: *"I am Santa Claus riding on the desk lamp."*

I'd only just begun saying this to myself when the woman
from that window looked up at me and said: "Bring me your
documents."

The line was perfectly quiet, probably thinking that I had
some kind of "special connections." One old granny did warn
me: "Well, when you go to the cashier, you'll just be in a long
line there instead."

This really didn't bother me, since *"I am Santa Claus riding on the desk lamp."* There was no one at all at the cashier's
window, and as I approached I thought: "The cashier must
be gone." But stepping up to the window, I saw her standing
right there.

Through all of January I was *"Santa Claus riding on the desk
lamp."* We managed to gather together the documents fairly
quickly, and finally my husband was ready to submit them. At
first they bounced him around here and there—this signature
wasn't right, or they didn't like that seal, always something.
Vadim supposed that they all just wanted money out of him.

I asked him: "Is it hard for you to pay out this money?"

"Yeah."

"Then I'll take over."

A torrent of esoteric names started bursting out of me—
names like "a pillow which bakes cakes" and "a stovepipe puff-
ing out caramels"—enough to rename half the city. Vadim
said that he didn't want to remember all these names, to
which I replied: "You don't even have to." My husband set
out immediately for his next attempt—all documents were
signed without delay.

They assigned us an apartment number, but we weren't able
to look at it yet—the building was still secured, and no one
was allowed in. I really wanted to see our new home, so, when

I went to bed that night, I said to myself: "You're a magician. Just have a look at the apartment in your dreams!"

I fell asleep. In a dream I was walking up to our new building and spoke to the security guard: "I want to look at Apartment 27."

"It's on the ninth floor, but take the stairs; the elevator isn't working."

I walked into the apartment, checked out the view from each window, and set off for the bathroom. At that point I woke up.

I told the dream to my husband and my friend. When I had finished, my friend asked: "What exactly are you saying? Were you awake when you were there? You described everything in so much detail!"

The three of us decided to see how accurate my description of the apartment really was. Walking up to the building, we saw the security guard washing his car. I came up with a name for him: "*he who embubliates his cariola.*" We asked him where the main entrance was. He sent us to the caretaker, who described our apartment to us in detail. It was exactly as in my dream, and, what's more, the caretaker described it using the same words I had.

My husband's mouth fell open in amazement, and he sputtered: "If you'd asked him to show us the apartment right away, he would have done it."

After that, whenever I need to resolve a particularly complex issue, I say to myself in bed "*I am a magician*" and fall asleep.

In April we received authorization to move in and got to spend the May Day holiday in our new apartment.

Everyday Life of Magicians

In this chapter we present stories from the everyday lives of magicians. The reader may wonder why, then, stories like "The Count on Ice Island" are included. After all, it's not like a million dollars suddenly fell out of the sky!

In the hustle and bustle of life, ever pursuing the illusions intrinsic to our worldview, we so often lose sight of the seemingly insignificant events around us. Obsessed by our personal problems, we simply don't pay attention to such "trifles" as a dog stranded on a floating block of ice or a short, chubby kid in a baseball cap (cf. "The Count on Ice Island"). This is how we lose our ability to perform miracles.

If we notice what is happening right here, right now, at this very moment, then the world becomes transformed—it begins to sparkle with fresh colors, to reveal its secrets. We can make generalizations which describe the state of soaring and still not be a single step closer to it. Meanwhile, the "door" leading to it is always cracked open; we need only be mindful and perceptive of everything occurring around us.

The Sultan of Brunei

> You should make decisions very quickly, especially
> those which seem the most bizarre, the most outland-
> ish: it is impossible to break free of the imposed course
> of events in any other way.
>
> Evgeny Kliuev—*Book of Ghosts*

I have a large family: my husband Fedor, an 18-year-old son
Anton, a daughter Liuba in sixth grade, our German Shepherd Nika, and a large, arrogant cat named Basia. A couple
years back, my husband wasn't working and was always lazing
around the house. No sooner did he finally manage to land
a position in a joint venture company than it fell apart. Two
months later, he was hired by a company which manufac-
tured specialized electronic equipment, but soon he was out
of work again—the director of the company fled the country
with all the company's money. After another long interval
without work, my husband found a position in a construction
company. After working there for six months, he still had not
received a single kopeck in pay, and when the country fell into
financial crisis, all the workers were laid off.

For all practical purposes, we lived exclusively on my salary.
My family's appetite didn't suffer a bit, though, and there was
never enough money. We were barely surviving from paycheck
to paycheck, gradually sinking into debt to our friends. We ate
only vegetables and grains, meat being a forbidden luxury.

At that time, I was attending various psychological work-shops, which also required money. This aggravated my family, especially my husband. He was constantly expressing his outrage: "You are cramming all this nonsense into your head, wasting our money on your stupid seminars."

Pressured by my husband, I stopped attending them. No longer able to participate in what I most liked to do, I fell into a deep depression and lost all interest in living. I felt weak, and my blood pressure plummeted to a critical level.

Right around then, my girlfriend took me to a magician's class. When I spoke about my troubles, they renamed me as *"the Sultan of Brunei joyfully dancing the tarantella with a colander on his head, surrounded by his entourage."* I knew as much about Brunei—what's more its Sultan—as I knew about the inhabitants of Alpha Centauri. One of the participants at the seminar told me that he was the richest man in the world. It was perfect.

Returning home in a fantastic mood, I firmly resolved to attend the two-day seminar in magic which was coming in two weeks. I couldn't care less where the money might come from. At home, I wrapped a "turban" made from a towel around my head, put a colander on top of it, and gathering together the entire family, broke into a lively dance. Naturally, in keeping with my new role, I had to be surrounded by my entourage!

My family watched this vigorous Italian dance with interest and sympathy. My husband, frowning, blurted out: "You don't need teaching; you need treatment."

My daughter exclaimed: "You could have at least lowered the blinds! People might have seen you from the street! What will I tell them?"

Despite the nasty comments, I felt an unusual elevation of spirit and an influx of strength after the dance. As if on wings,

I started flying around the house: I "licked clean" the entire apartment, prepared lunch, and ironed the linen. At about 12:30 that night, I still couldn't stop.

I was overcome with curiosity about who this Sultan of Brunei really was. I read in an Encyclopedia that Brunei is a small country on the northwest coast of the island of Kalimantan. Two days later, I came upon a magazine called *Vacationing!* Opening it up, I found a picture of the Brunei monarch surrounded by his numerous wives and other relatives with an article about his incalculable wealth. Wow! What an amazing support signal that was!

It turns out that Sultan Haji Hassanal Bolkiah is considered the richest man in the world. It is estimated that he is worth about $40 billion. The Sultan's huge palace has 1,788 sumptuous rooms and a fleet of 170 limousines and 530 other luxury automobiles.

It was two days before the seminar and there was still no money for it, but still I didn't give up. My standing in the family had already been damaged, so I had to keep going to the end.

After work, I'd wear the colander on my head and dance the tarantella till I dropped. I responded with dignity to the sarcastic comments of my family, as becomes a monarch. I would say: "Even Queen Elizabeth II of Great Britain treats the Sultan of Brunei with great respect."

On the day before the seminar, when I arrived at work, they were handing out our paychecks in advance—and what's more, with a substantial bonus which no one had expected.

After the seminar I decided that it was time to take on my husband. He had completely lost interest in work and just hung around all day at home, abusing me out of spite. First, I wrote out this retelling in "I":

I wait for manna from heaven while skimping on pennies. I don't know myself, why I look down so much on household chores. I don't do anything, nor let me live in peace, and then I lie down and feel sick. What if I went on strike? I'm angry at me; sometimes I feel like whacking me across the head, so that my brain will click into place and start working again. I look at me and think: "Why do I sabotage everything I do?" And I realized that I feel that I don't value me enough. Once, when I was in a good mood, I admitted to myself: "My pride is wounded; after all, I am developing more than me. I should be smarter, and therefore feel inadequate."

I composed a new retelling in "I" every day, accumulating a whole stack of them. I also searched my imagination for the right name for Fedor: *"I am the cat chasing a mouse."*

A week later my husband landed a job for a one-month trial period. I was concerned whether they would actually pay him in the end.

One evening I was coming home from work with my girlfriend. The commuter train was late. Suddenly I noticed a cat lazily climbing down from the platform and making its way through the deep snow.

My girlfriend was surprised: "Why do you think it went onto the snow?"

"Because it had to," I answered.

At that moment the cat jumped out from under the platform, a mouse desperately scurrying along in front of it. The striped hunter excitedly pursued its booty. Finally it pounced. Lifting the mouse up in its teeth, it leisurely went on its way. Right then the commuter train appeared.

Inspired by this remarkable sign, I arrived home. Fedor wasn't there, and I asked the children where he was. Liuba told me that at five o'clock that evening his work called and asked him to come in for his paycheck. About an hour later, my proud husband appeared with his "booty."

Fedor was happy with his new job. He was paid regularly and, although we haven't yet acquired 170 limousines, we do have everything we need in this life. And Fedor is no longer bothered by my odd behavior.

Riding Doggyback

It looked like a difficult day ahead: I had to finish sewing a jumper, apply for a new job, attend a meeting at our firm, and drop off several orders to clients. I got up at six that morning, prepared breakfast, and fed my son. The thought suddenly struck me: "I have to do something! Or else I'll never get it all done."

Right then my dog, Lassie, ran into the room, and I re-named myself: *"I am the one who will get there on time on the back of my very own dog."* I stuck in the words "very own" on purpose to give it a nice rhythm.

The thought kept spinning through my head: "Who can help me out? Maybe my husband will give me a ride into town."

My husband is a "square." He does everything most meticulously, and everything is always in its place. I thought about how best to appeal to him and, as he was eating breakfast, I entered the kitchen saying:

> The crawdads were tired of waiting around
> For beer lovers to come through the fog.
> *I am the one who will get there on time*
> *On the back of my very own dog.*

My spouse remained silent.

> Scrubbing the cow in a yellow tuxedo,
> By evening the loofah was soggy.

172

I am the one who will get there on time
On the back of my very own doggy.

My husband looked up at me intrigued and asked: "What do you want, dear?"

I probably wanted it overly much,
While dreaming alone in the bog.
I am the one who will get there on time
On the back of my very own dog.

"So what did you want in the bog?"

I told him about everything I had to do that day, exclaiming in the end: "Somehow I've got to get it all done on time!"

"No, I will not take out the car today. Bring the jumper with you and sew on the sleeves at the meeting."

I was working fervently on the jumper when, hearing the time on the radio, I realized that I would be late for the bus.

"I'll make it. After all, I managed to write those amazing verses!" I thought. I sat down to enjoy a cup of tea, leisurely dressed, and left my apartment. I didn't worry about how I was going to get to the other side of the city—I was overflowing with new verse:

Roasting like herrings packed snug in a pie
Being cooked on a fiery log,
I am the one who will get there on time
On the back of my very own dog.

Right then a friend's car pulled up next to me. He stuck out his head and called out: "Do you want a ride? I can take you as far as the bridge."

"That's right where I'm going; I can catch a bus from there."

The conductor on the bus kept ignoring me, so I didn't impose myself on her. When I arrived to apply for my new job, I blurted out to these people I had never seen before in my life:

> I probably wanted it overly much,
> While dreaming alone in the bog.
> *I am the one who will get there on time*
> *On the back of my very own dog.*

No one seemed to mind. The manager wasn't in his office right then, and I couldn't wait. I liked the "loofah" verse very much and repeated it, inquiring: "Can't we just do this after the holiday?"

"That would be fine."

I arrived at the meeting on time. A surprise awaited me there: in honor of International Women's Day, the head of our local government had decided to sponsor a star-studded concert for women. Our company had been assigned two tickets, which were to be given away by lottery. I instantly composed a quatrain:

> The sweet-singing chick flew up into the sky,
> After filling the gas tanks with grog.
> *I am the one who will get there on time*
> *On the back of my very own dog.*

I pulled out the first lucky lottery ticket, and the second one went to my friend. Not long before I had given her the book *The Art of Soaring* to read. She winked at me knowingly: "Your shamanism, no doubt?"

I managed to complete all my other errands and out of sheer joy composed:

> The goat became tired of bleating morosely,
> Her marriage had gone to the dogs.
> *I am the one who will get there on time*
> *On the back of my very own dog.*

That entire day I had been so busy composing verses that there had been no time to think about my problems, and that's why everything worked out perfectly!

Apartment for Sale

My husband and I work as real estate agents. For two months we had been trying to sell a very nice apartment. There just weren't any clients; no one even wanted to look at it. The apartment's owner, Margarita, was furious when she called us one day: "What's with you two? Don't you need the money?!" At that point I remembered that I'm a magician and applied the technique of imaginative renaming: *"I am the one who trains giraffes to read and write in Spanish."*

Leaving the office that afternoon, I decided to test the waters: if there is a dark-green car to the left of the entrance, and a white car to the right, then we should put an advertisement on cable television. I don't know why I thought this—in general, we consider that television is overly expensive and not that effective. As I was leaving the building, I immediately saw a dark-green Zhiguli Model 10 on the street to the left, but there was no sign of a white car anywhere. Then out of the corner of my eye I caught sight of a white Zhiguli Model 6 to the right, partly hidden from me by the door.

The next morning I set out to buy advertising on cable television. The very moment I paid them, I received this message on my pager: "Client wants to look at Margarita's apartment."

Twenty minutes later I met a young couple—a rather gloomy man and a provocatively dressed woman. Soon afterwards we were greeted at the door by a very agitated Margarita. The man, who was named Dmitry, stayed in the entryway, but the woman walked in, glanced over everything in less than a minute and was done.

Margarita fell into despair: "That's not a client! What a way to look at an apartment! I can't take this anymore—I'm sick of it. I have a migraine and pains in my chest."

With a conspiratorial look, I whispered quietly to her: "Do you *really* want to sell this apartment?"

"Yes," she whispered back.

"Then don't get hysterical. Instead just say over and over: *'I am the one who trains giraffes to read and write in Spanish.'*"

"But what does it mean?"

"I won't explain anything, but if you repeat this phrase, you will sell the apartment."

At that point Margarita offered me a cup of coffee. About ten minutes later, as I was preparing to leave, she happily announced: "You know what? My headache is gone, and my chest pain has stopped, too."

At home my husband wrote this poem:

> I'm often called a "gentleman,"
> My love for her won't vanish.
> *I'm the one who trains giraffes*
> *To read and write in Spanish.*

I liked it very much, and it spun around my head all evening long.

The next day at exactly nine o'clock in the morning, Dmitry called and said: "I want to buy that apartment. I'll put down a deposit today."

The sale was closed in an incredibly short period of time.

The Hat

My son Gennady had been coughing violently for an entire month. Yet he flatly refused to wear a hat during the winter. He was now a senior in college, but ever since the eighth grade, I'd been trying to get across to him that he had to wear a warm hat in freezing weather.

Right after a magician's seminar, I resolved to move from words to action. I came home and, since no one was there, put down this retelling in "I":

"I won't wear a hat."

"I'll get sick and cough a lot."

"I look stupid in a hat."

"Small hats look good on me; they're stylish."

"None of my friends wear hats."

"Well, normal people do wear hats; the others end up in hospitals."

"My hair gets all mussed under a hat."

"My haircut is short on top with a tiny 'lawn' in front— there is nothing to get messed up."

"Oh, get off it! It's not even cold outside."

"Hey! Look out the window! This isn't Africa!"

"I just want me to be warm, comfortable, and healthy during the winter."

As soon as I finished writing this, I heard the front door open. My son shouted excitedly: "Mom, I bought a hat!"

Even though Gennady started wearing a hat, his cough didn't go away. At the next magician's class, I spoke about this and was renamed *"a boa constrictor which condenses with its tail."* A magician gave me the image of a boa constrictor which, flicking its tail into a can of condensed milk, lifts it to its mouth and licks off the sweet milk.

At home I made a tail out of packing tape, attaching it to my bathrobe behind my tail bone. Then I opened a can of condensed milk and placed it on the table. With quick movements, I flicked my tail into the can and, raising it to my mouth, licked off the sweet milk. I performed this ritual every morning.

I molded a boa constrictor and an open "can" out of modeling clay and brought them to work, pouring a little correction fluid into the can. Even to this day, the "sculpture" sits on my work desk, arousing the curiosity of passersby.

Several days later my son stopped coughing completely.

The Lid with a Tiny Knob

For a while I've been attending classes in magic with my son, Misha. At first he was skeptical about "all that nonsense," but one day he had no choice but to resort to it.

On Wednesday Misha came home from school very dejected. His chemistry teacher, Petr Kondratievich, had called him up to the blackboard in the final minute of class. Misha somehow managed to write out the formula but couldn't name the reaction type. In the end he was saved by the bell, but his relief turned out to be premature. Petr Kondratievich informed him that at the next lesson he would question Misha about the main topic—the oxidation reaction. His next chemistry lesson was on Thursday, so he had just one day to prepare himself for the impossible. He could only hope for a miracle. Misha wrote out a letter retelling the situation in "I."

"Throughout the entire chemistry lesson, I was afraid that I would call me up to the blackboard and, as ill luck would have it, this finally happened at the very last moment. I asked me to name the type of reaction, and I became confused, but in the end I was saved by the bell. I promised that at the next lesson I would ask me about the main topic. *Oh, how I wish I'd forget to call me up to the blackboard.*"

Misha wrote this key phrase on another piece of paper and put it into his schoolbag.

The next morning he decided to test the waters, setting up these conditions: "If NTV is showing when I turn the TV on, then everything will turn out great." Misha switched on the television, and as it turned out the NTV channel was broadcasting the program "For Future Use." A respectable-looking man, holding a yellow butter dish, was stating how important it is to store butter in the refrigerator in a dish with a lid to keep its surface from oxidizing. The program ended, and a caption appeared on the screen stating that the speaker was a chemistry professor.

We rushed off to find a lid with a tiny knob like the one on TV. We did find two similar lids, but they were clear. We covered the butter in the refrigerator with one of them, and Misha put the other one into his schoolbag. Then he set off for school.

Returning home that afternoon, he was beaming with joy. Petr Kondratievich had given the class a test which Misha managed to finish easily. True, he did have a little trouble with the final equation. His lab partner helped him out, and that piece of paper with the key phrase proved useful—the last equation was solved on it. Misha got an "A" on the test!

The lid with the tiny knob has now become an object of power in our home. Each morning I take it out of the refrigerator and put it in my son's book bag and, as soon as he gets home after school, he puts it back into the refrigerator. If Misha is poorly prepared for a lesson, and the teacher glances into the grade book to find someone to call on, my son pronounces the key phrase, and usually his teacher will call on someone else. Misha has begun to do better in all his classes and has a lot of fun playing with magic.

The Schoolmarm

My 18-year-old son, Timofey, was attending college. His mathematics teacher, Polina Vasilievna, was constantly finding fault with him.

"Sit up straight! Why are you all hunched over? Don't cock your head like that!"

She didn't seem to notice the other students but tormented Timofey mercilessly. Whenever Polina called him up to the blackboard, she could hardly contain her sarcasm.

"Look at him acting like a big Hollywood star!"

Timofey ended up with a "C" in math, not because he didn't know the material, but because the teacher would pick apart his work for the most trivial details.

Polina always looked very unkempt, like she had forty Cossacks on her tail. She dressed in clashing colors—a red blouse, bright-yellow jacket, green skirt, purple scarf, brown tights, and white shoes. To top it off, she would put on lipstick which didn't go with anything. Timofey would often say that she was "a true sight to behold."

I advised him to retell the situation in "I," and this is what he came up with:

At college I'm always finding fault with me: "Don't sit like that! Stop whistling!" not noticing that I myself am a true sight to behold. First, I never prepare for class, and then I start picking on me. I tell me that I look half-asleep, but how am I supposed to look—at this time of morning?

I may be lazy, but is being a workaholic any better? I can't be straight with me. But no way can I cheat myself either—I see right through me. Maybe I even like me a little, and that's why I give so much attention to me?

After writing this retelling, my son announced: "I need to do something to make Polina feel better. I'll dress up; she'll like that."

In college male students are required to wear suits, but in reality they just hang around in denim jackets. So the next day Timofey wore a stylish shirt, suit coat, and tie. He captured Polina's heart forever. The mathematics teacher was most taken by his silver tie, which shimmered with mother-of-pearl and magnificently matched his gray suit.

Completely smitten, she announced in front of the entire class: "Timofey, today you are *elegance itself!*"

To receive that kind of approval from this forbidding teacher was completely unheard of, and Timofey, stunned, suddenly felt like a real man. My son began to buy ties and has become astute at picking them out. Now he changes his tie every two days, not for the sake of other people's opinion of him, but for the satisfaction of feeling his own self-worth.

Polina now helps Timofey come up with the answer in class, always gives him "A's" and "B's," and encourages others to follow his example.

Once my son admitted: "I never thought that a schoolmarm could give you hints. I'm even beginning to kind of like her. After all, because of her, I've learned to dress with class."

Timofey's respectable outer appearance also attracted girls majoring in management. They began flocking around him. He only has to appear in the school corridors, and enraptured admirers swoop down on him from all directions.

Recently my son asked me for a book on astrology to give to Polina. She was fascinated by astrology and once, after calculating the coming of some eclipse, she canceled all her classes and went to Novgorod to view it.

After that Timofey said: "To be honest, I didn't understand a single word of that book, but Polina found something she liked and has thanked me for it many times over."

Conversations with Animals

In the middle of April, I set out for my "hacienda." The last time I had been at my summerhouse was the end of October, and I wondered: "Will the lock be snapped off? The shutters forced open? The windows smashed?"

In past years our summerhouse had been robbed during the winter. Thieves would sneak into the house and steal all kinds of things—once they even broke all the glass. Sweeping up the shards, I recalled from my childhood how some school friends and I had broken a bunch of windows with makeshift air guns. We had constructed the guns from bicycle pumps and thick elastic straps which shot homemade lead bullets. My close friend could make anything and put together a particularly remarkable gun. In the evenings we would climb up onto the roof of his apartment building and shoot at the windows of a neighboring building about fifty yards away. We got so excited whenever we heard the sound of a breaking window, and with trepidation we would peer through binoculars to see what happened! Obviously, I had to rename this episode in my life.

In 1993, I discovered magic and decided once and for all to deal with the problem of vandalism—I would leave a "sentry"*

---

* There is a very effective technique which creates a helper to help resolve a problem. An example of how to do this is given in this story. Any object can be used as a helper—from people to animals to slippers or even a hot water heater (cf. "Moving").

at the summerhouse. I thanked Vanya for warning me that our summerhouse could be broken into and the glass broken every year. What's more, our Moscow apartment might start being vandalized as well. Some dark night a band of vicious cutthroats could break into our home and drive us half-naked into the street with nothing to our name. I offered to Vanya a large, blue sphere which emitted dazzling white shafts of light.

Now I had to find a sentry. I addressed the summerhouse with the request to nominate potential candidates. My glance fell on a fork with a beautiful plastic handle. The only spoons and forks which remained after the robberies were aluminum, but this one was real stainless steel. I solemnly addressed the fork, explaining my situation, and gave it the gift of a little hippopotamus in a blue uniform. Then I proposed that it enter into honorable service as the summerhouse sentry. I further expounded on how interesting its life would become—previously it had just slumbered sluggishly through the entire winter, but now it could lead an active life—exposing the secret intrigues of potential thieves and conducting educational and outreach work with them. My proposal was gladly accepted, and we "came to an understanding"—the fork would periodically send forth blue balloons (the gift to Vanya), which would neatly hover over each picket of the fence around our yard. I promised the fork that in return I'd keep it forever and would amiably chat with it during my visits—in fact, not that different from what a man promises his sweetheart when declaring his love.

The fork has performed its duty faithfully—for three years now no one has attempted to break into our house. The fact that the fork is indeed the sentry was confirmed while I was typing up this story. My son came into the room and turned on the television. The broadcast was about a man who collects

knives and forks. Whenever he visits anyone, he looks for unusual forks, checking the brand on their handles!

As I approached my summerhouse, I could see from a
distance that the lock was hanging intact, and the plywood
which I had nailed over the windows was in place. Entering the yard, I felt my usual irritation at seeing a chicken
in my current bushes breakfasting on worms. In the spring,
the melting snow undermines our fence, and chickens "discover" doorways into my precious garden. Usually I just grab
a couple clumps of clay and throw them at the chickens, scaring them away. As they leave, they reveal the holes under the
fence which I can then plug up. Out here in the countryside,
chickens are considered to be pretty stupid birds; there's even
a saying: "a fool of a hen," which refers to the more well-
known saying: "a fool of a woman." So, oftentimes after you
throw a glob of clay at the chickens, they start rushing around
in panic, completely forgetting everything in the world and,
in particular, that passage through which they entered the
garden. Cackling loudly, they try to fly over the fence, which
exasperates their owners.

Essentially, we are not that different from these fussy birds.
We have forgotten how we wound up in this world, through
which gap in the fabric of the Universe we found our way
here. In confusion we rush around the garden beds our entire
lives as we seek a few tasty worms, trying to dodge the painful
blows of dirt clods, in the hope of discovering some way out,
to return from whence we came.

After this "epiphany," I performed a magical dance for the
chicken. I made amusing movements with my body (if anyone had seen me, they would have thought I was crazy) and
at the end uttered the mantra—FIRANUZH. The effect was
astounding. The chicken was about eighty feet from me, and

it obviously was not aware of my presence. As soon as I began my "conversation," it stopped raking the earth with its claws and unexpectedly set off straight towards me. When it had covered about a third of the distance, the chicken turned, approached the fence, quickly found the hole, and casually left the yard. I was dumbfounded. A wave of joy swept over me, as I thought to myself: "It really worked!"

At that moment I heard some excited crowing and flapping of wings on the other side of the fence. Peering over the gate, I saw two cocks fighting. One was a hefty, well-seasoned rooster, and the other a lean, younger one. Again I started repeating FIRANUZH. Instantly, the young rooster jumped back from his more experienced adversary, who stood there nonplussed, unable to comprehend what was happening. Then with solemn dignity the roosters went their own ways. A police captain who happened to be passing by remarked that the brawlers had separated because they saw his uniform, but I knew the real reason.

I went off to tend my garden in a highly elevated state of consciousness. That evening, as I was walking to the railroad platform, I saw a cat making its way along the road: "I should try to communicate with it, too." I decided not to dance or pronounce the mantra out loud, so as not to attract the attention of passersby. I named it MICHUZEN. I had hardly begun repeating this mantra, when the cat suddenly stopped short in bewilderment, sniffed all around, and started slowly padding towards me. About ten feet away, it sat down under a tree and, looking first at me, then at the sun, started meticulously preening itself. As the cat rapturously licked its raised front paw, it reminded me of a tiny person waving his hand at me. The cat's behavior dispelled any last doubts I might have had that the episode with the chickens had been accidental.

The Count on Ice Island

One warm April evening, I found ashes on the elbow rest of my armchair. I confronted my thirteen-year-old son, and he admitted that he had been smoking cigarettes. Right at that point, the strains of a song floated up from the street: "It seems that we're not meant to be, it seems that we're not meant to be; there's no love between us, there's no love between us; it seems that, it seems that you've been cheating on me, you've been cheating on me... " This felt like a support signal and, singing these simple words, I set out for a walk.

Spring was definitely late that year. In the beginning of April, so much snow fell in Moscow in one day that it seemed it wouldn't be gone until summer. When I went to visit my mother on her birthday in the middle of April, it was twenty-three degrees Fahrenheit (-5 °C). I couldn't remember it ever being that cold before. But everything was set right by two days of rain, which unexpectedly washed away almost all the snow. Still it was hardly warm, and at night the puddles would freeze.

Like a capricious young girl, the spring kept surprising me. In the last week of April, warm weather finally settled in. Everyone, gladdened by the change, switched to leather and denim jackets and sweaters, and young people were even parading about in T-shirts with colorful images and inscriptions in English.

189

After waiting so long for the warm weather, people came out to stroll in the local park. All along the asphalt paths, teenagers raced about on rollerblades, bicycles, skateboards, motorcycles, and mopeds. Everywhere resounded a cacophony of sounds—dogs barking, children shouting, birds singing, all interspersed with the rollicking songs of old drunken men.

I went out in jeans and a T-shirt, but, stepping into a strong wind, I reconsidered my decision: "Is it worth going back for my jacket?" Seeing two poodles trotting out from the entryway, looking like miniature lambs, I intrepidly set out for the park. On the way I performed the exercise of "dreaming while awake." I imagined that I was sleeping, and any signal from the outer world was miraculously transformed into a character of a dream, into an imaginary form.

I "woke up" only when I came up to the divided highway at the front of the park. A traffic jam about a half mile long completely blocked one direction, and an uninterrupted flow of "iron horses" rushed by at a frenzied pace in the other. Such congestion on this road was unusual. My glance fell on an old police booth, looking good with its newly-painted, plastered walls. I moved towards the nearest traffic signal about four hundred yards away, mentally *plastering and painting the walls*.

Crossing the road at the signal, I came to a large pond surrounded by concrete slabs. In the past, there had been a boat dock on this pond. When I was a young boy, I used to come here and pretend to be a sailor plying the heavy oars. On the northern bank of the pond was the expansive manor of Count Sheremetiev, now a museum surrounded by an imposing iron fence with sharp-pointed spikes. Formerly, there had been no fence. I used to love to ride my bicycle along the avenues of the old park, wheeling around the sculpture of naked Venus, and flying past the Dutch villa and conservatory. Sometimes I would stop in at the palace to admire the interesting exhibits inside. I liked slipping the felt slippers, about size 14, over my boots, softly sliding along the waxed parquet floor. In particular, I remember the huge carved table. On its surface was a highly detailed map made from different types of wood depicting the manor grounds with the pond and all the buildings.

The luxurious palace and lofty chapel had recently been repainted in a delicate pink.

My route passed along the southern bank of the pond. A boy in glasses, about ten years old, was sitting on the concrete slab surrounded by a group of children daring him to jump into the water. The boy took off his boots, rolled up his jeans, and, to the exuberant cries of his audience, lowered his bare legs into the freezing water. "It's going to his head," I thought and concocted this formula for the daredevil: *"I am a Zhiguli Model 8 car hitched to a jerking stopper."*

Before long I reached a long, narrow canal which emptied into the pond directly opposite the palace. In contrast to the pond which was completely free of ice, almost the entire canal was covered over with a gray, porous ice; only a small fringe of water about seven feet wide stretched along the edges. Several heavy chunks of wood lay on top of the icy monolith—some ancient trees in the park had been cut down, and the local kids, probably, had wanted to test the solidity of the "iceberg." The thought came to me that, if I took a running start and jumped right next to the logs, the ice might even hold out.

At that point I heard a protracted howl and discovered that my thought had been manifested—a German Shepherd was standing on the ice in the middle of the canal. Its owner was commanding it from the bank: "Count, come!" but the dog only howled mournfully and barked in protest. It seemed completely discouraged—if it obeyed its master, then at some point its front paws might break through the ice into the water. The dog didn't realize that it could simply leap over to the shore. Many onlookers had gathered on both banks of the canal, bearing witness to the fact that the Count had been on its icy island for quite some time. Advice poured forth from all sides, both to the German Shepherd and to its master:

"Just jump, you stupid dog!"

"C'mon, you can swim across! It's no big deal!"

"Why don't you build a log bridge for the mutt?"

"Go to the other side; the ice is closer to the bank there."

Moving along the canal, I started dancing, unnoticed by people around, repeating the mantra CHUSINUR for the Count. Almost immediately a support signal appeared—two huge Rottweilers crossed the bridge over the canal. As they marched along dignified without leashes, it seemed that it was actually the dogs who were walking the two teenagers accompanying them. I set out behind them along the opposite bank of the canal—there lay the furthest point on my route. On the other side, some boys were dragging over a good-sized log, and the dog's owner went to help them.

At that moment a loud croaking could be heard. Looking up, I saw a large raven perched on a nearby tree, observing the developing events with interest. Glancing around, I noticed that the number of curious ravens was no less than the number of humans (including your humble servant). The ravens were commenting with interest on the various twists and turns of the unfolding spectacle.

Reaching the spot where the canal flowed into the pond, I hesitated: "Now the boys will drag a second log over, and the Count will be safely rescued from its captivity." But intuition told me that the whole affair had to be brought to its final denouement—I had to see with my own eyes that everything would turn out well. So I headed back to the bridge. Coming towards me was a nice-looking woman in a tailored suit and an unusual black hat with a gray satin band. The hat was spherical and resembled a military helmet, but, this said, it actually looked quite spectacular. I realized that freeing the prisoner must have reached the decisive stage but didn't turn around to see what was happening. I kept intoning CHUSINUR.

I heard snuffling behind me—those same two Rottweilers had again overtaken me, their muscles rippling under their glistening coats. Only at that point did I allow myself to look back. The Count, whimpering and whining, had begun its courageous passage across the log bridge. Suddenly it slipped, plopping right down into the water. The owner managed to seize the dog by a paw, which kept it from lunging back. At that point the Count realized that it was just standing in water, and that it could easily wade across the remaining distance.

A burst of applause, congratulatory shouts, and approving raven croaks burst forth, and the spectators began to disperse. Our hero ran up to the nearest oak tree, sniffed all around, and amply wetted it, lifting its hind leg high. Then it trotted off happily down the path, as if nothing had happened.

Turning back towards home, I noticed that the wind had died down completely. In front of me, a girl of about seven was leading her three-year-old brother by the hand. He was trying to break free and take off his baseball cap.

The girl turned the bill of the hat backwards and said: "You're so cool! All cool people wear their baseball caps backwards!"

"Yeah, I'm cool," the kid agreed, no longer trying to pull away his hand.

Marveling at her masterful renaming, I started imitating the little boy, repeating several times: "Yeah, I'm cool!"

I had already begun composing a plan for this story in my mind and, approaching the stoplight, realized that the grand finale should be the absence of any traffic jam on the highway. My hopes were not realized—the congestion was only slightly less.

I crossed the road, figuring that it's really OK to stretch the truth a little for effect—surely in literary works you can't manage without it. Looking back at the street, I couldn't believe my eyes—the traffic jam had completely vanished. I had no idea how it could possibly have disappeared in so short a time.

Approaching my home, I met a reddish-brown mutt, whose ancestors were most likely lapdogs. Rusty just sat there, attentively watching me from under its "bangs" which flopped down over its eyes filled with deep respect for me.

That evening my son assured me that he would quit smoking. More than half a year has passed, and I haven't found any signs of smoking anywhere.

The Cake

It was an overcast autumn day. I was sitting at the computer, typing up the text of yet another magical story. Music was playing softly—I felt like I was on the edge of nothingness. At that moment, the door into my room burst open, and my wife hurled a question at me which actually sounded more like an accusation: "Did you eat the cake?"

It was in fact true. Late last night, guests had come to our house with a cake. My son, Nikita, had been asleep and was not able to share the delicacy. By the way, he really likes cakes, as do I. We saved Nikita about a third of the cake—three full-fledged pieces. The next morning, he ate the cake for breakfast, leaving a single piece. For lunch I snacked on a pair of bananas and finished up the cake. Then I sat down at the computer, and there appeared my wife, fuming at the door of my room.

"Um, yeah," I forced myself to say with a note of despair in my voice, as if I'd been caught in the act of performing some horrible transgression.

"Have you no conscience, papa! Couldn't you leave the last piece for your child?!"

The door slammed closed. Instantly, a memory flashed through my mind, how as a kid I was so happy whenever a cake appeared in our home. Usually I would try to make it last, always saving that final slice for the next day. How warm my heart would feel, knowing that there was still one more sweet piece left in the refrigerator!

But the matter was done; the cake was gone. My mind, trying to salvage my reputation, recalled that just yesterday I had brought home two pounds of chocolate cookies which, perhaps, might have been even more tasty than the ill-fated cake. This was followed by the banal idea of running to the store to buy another cake before my son arrived home.

In the end, I thought better of it: but what about magic? My glance naturally moved towards the window, where I caught sight of a pigeon gliding down to the overhang above the entrance to our building. Next I noticed a large plastic bag caught on some wires connecting the antenna on the roof of our nine-story building with a small one-story building on the opposite side of the street—the former Municipal Housing Committee Office. This bag was fluttering about forty feet above the ground resembling a kite. I received my name: *"I am the one who attaches the plastic bag to the wires."*

At 5:00 that afternoon, Yulia was scheduled to come visit me. She was in deep depression from "inextricable" problems in her personal life. She had come to me before, and I had managed to help her. In general, Yulia is a very talented woman, helps her friends with their own issues, and once even saved a friend's husband from alcoholism, but she was unable to help herself. I have tried so many times to explain the simplest magical techniques to her, but our meetings usually ended up like this. First, Yulia would speak nonstop about the issues troubling her, repeating herself often and not listening to anything I'd say. If I did manage to get a few words in, she would interrupt me after a few sentences and continue articulating her inner ruminations. All I could do was to silently rename her, and at the end of the meeting give her a magical name, which did not always help due to her reluctance to incorporate magic into her worldview.

At about 4:30, a friend called and said that he wanted to come over within the hour. He didn't mind that Yulia would be there. "I'm stopping by just for a couple minutes," he said. Soon thereafter he arrived with this gigantic cake, probably weighing about six pounds, in an unbelievably large, round cardboard box. Handing this surprise over to me, he instantly "vanished," promising to drop by with his wife that evening.

Yulia's visit proceeded according to the scenario described above. From time to time, I pronounced in my mind: *"I am the one who sparkles purple in the crystal vase."* This name, discovered over a year ago, had helped her recover a huge sum of money. Toward the end of our visit, Yulia had calmed down somewhat, and with some trepidation I decided to give her an old draft manuscript of several magical stories: "Who knows? Maybe it'll help!"

My son was impatiently waiting for me in the kitchen: "What's in that big box?" he asked, trying to feign indifference. In order to strengthen his belief in the unlimited power of magic, I told him the spectacular story about how the cake had appeared. Nikita proclaimed that this magic affected him as much as the time the lost cat was found at a forest camp.*

Nikita could no longer pretend that he didn't care about what was in the box. His eyes flashed with irresistible desire: "Let's open it and take a look!" It was nine o'clock in the evening. I didn't know when my friend would come, or if he'd come at all, so I gave him the go-ahead.

With bated breath Nikita lifted the lid. Yes! His hopes had been justified—a masterpiece of culinary art lay in the box before him. First off was the size—both its diameter and height were staggering. The top was decorated with creamy

* Cf. the story "Seminar in the Woods."

rosettes—orange and bright scarlet—with green leaves interspersed with slender white "veins" like coral. All this lay on a thick layer of delicious, white frosting. The inside of this delicacy consisted primarily of meringue and nuts. Neither Nikita, my wife, nor I had ever seen such a colossus. It was obvious once we had opened the box that it would be impossible not to cut a piece for Nikita.

At about 10:00 that evening, our friend arrived with his wife, and we drank tea and ate cake together. Suddenly the telephone rang. When I picked up the receiver, I didn't immediately realize what was happening. I heard a voice exclaim: "It worked!!!" At first I was confused but then recognized Yulia's voice. As it turned out, while on her way home, she had read nearly all the stories (about twenty pages) and was trying out the technique of giving thanks. Yulia lives far from the subway station, and to reach her home she has to take either the bus, which doesn't run very often, or the shuttle, which only operates until 8:00 in the evening.

When Yulia had been at my place earlier, she had a cold and looked very feverish. She thanked Vanya for warning her that, if she had to wait too long for the bus, she could become chilled and seriously ill. Yulia offered a gift to Vanya, and at the subway station exit found two empty shuttle buses waiting for her. This so inspired Yulia that, arriving home, she wolfed down two bowls of soup, even though she hadn't been hungry at all in the subway and had hardly eaten for five days.

Magical transportation stories have become completely commonplace. I have heard them in various versions from scores of people. But from Yulia, sick and worn-out, I hadn't expected this at all.

Lady Napoleon

Not far from my house, next to the produce market and various hole-in-the-wall businesses, is a small plaza always crowded with people. At the end of winter, while walking past this tiny square, I would often run into a homeless woman of about forty-five years old, always drunk. Her bloated face was covered with bruises, her messy hair blew wildly in the wind, and her clothes were no more than tattered, old, greasy rags. Usually she'd be in the midst of some raucous scene with passersby or her drinking buddies.

Whenever I saw this homeless woman, I'd always give her a new name: *"I am the one who artistically blows my nose,"* *"I am the one who blinks like a neon sign,"* etc. She then completely disappeared for a while. The next time I saw her, I couldn't believe my eyes—she was stone-cold sober, and without her usual black eye. Elated by my success, I shared this joyful news with my wife. At first she didn't share my jubilation, answering: "You're always making a mountain out of a molehill. She probably just didn't have any money for booze, so she was sober."

But before long my wife had changed her mind, having seen for herself the homeless woman freed from the grip of the demon drink. Now she deftly wielded a hefty broom. The instrument literally flew around in her hands, like an artist's brush tracing broad sweeping strokes over a canvas. Passersby, glancing warily at the "artist," gave her wide berth, passing by a good ten feet away.

Several days later, the sweeper woman appeared before me again. This time her ensemble was adorned by a new feature which upstaged even the broom. Instead of her usual ragged skirt, under her nylon jacket she was wearing thick, nearly opaque tights with a most bizarre pattern. Huge red and yellow flowers, like orchids, stood out brightly on a dark background. The design resembled a Khokhloma wood painting. Although somewhat worn, the tights had not lost their charm.

I'd never seen such a work of art before and concluded that these unique tights had probably been custom made, possibly by some top designer in Paris. From that time on, those outlandish tights became a permanent attribute—they could be seen on her not only in the chill of February but also on a sultry afternoon in July.

By summer the former vagrant had become completely transformed. She began dressing more fashionably, preferring the contemporary style of young people: white gym shoes, her flowered tights, teen-style tee-shirt, denim miniskirt, jacket, and Panama hat. The brim of the hat was pulled up and pinned to the top. In a word—she was a true Lady Napoleon. My better half was delighted by these changes, exclaiming: "What a distinguished lady she has become! She seems younger, her face looks smoother, and her figure is truly a sight to behold."

I'd usually run into Lady Napoleon several times a day, and the small plaza where she wielded her broom from sunrise to sunset was always perfectly clean. Previously, the local drunks would all hang out there, but now they were loathe to mess with Lady Napoleon. God help anyone she saw drinking on her territory. She would attack them with her broom, declaring: "You can just march right out of here; now move it!" She had become a very strict woman and the genuine proprietress of the plaza. The people living in the area came to respect her, and many greeted her every morning.

Since then, Lady Napoleon has become an effective support signal for me: if I come across the "flowered tights," it means that the blessings of Lady Luck are assured for that day.

Every once in a while I recall the magical formula *"Bonaparte in flowered tights,"* and in very special cases I'll even put on thick, dark tights, on which my wife has meticulously appliquéd thick-stemmed garlands of large, bright yellow flowers around each leg.

The Magical Medal

On the eighth of May,* at six o'clock in the evening, I was returning home from work. Coming out of the "Paveletskaya" subway station, I headed for the ticket window in the commuter train depot. As I entered the hall where the ticket windows are located, I was met by total pandemonium. Even though four windows were serving customers, long lines of at least thirty people stretched back from each of them. I had never seen it like this in all the years I'd been going there—usually there were no more than three or four people waiting in line for tickets.

Completely bewildered, I entered the hall. I figured that the reason for such chaos was that it was the day before a holiday, and people were leaving the city in droves. The time had come for magic.

I caught sight of a young woman with long, slender legs in an unbelievably short skirt. She rushed past me, her high heels clicking crisply against the floor. That was it—the signal which would lead me out of this difficult situation. *"I am the one with clicking high heels!"* Stamping my soles against the asphalt (and all but charging after the possessor of the clicking heals), I decided to go without a ticket, all the more so because my train was leaving in just three minutes.

I walked out toward the train, pushing my way through the dense crowd. I was afraid that the platform might be blocked

* The eve of Victory Day, celebrated in Russia to commemorate the surrender of Nazi Germany. [trans]

off by ticket inspectors, allowing only those with tickets to pass, and I wouldn't be able to get through. At that point a round-bellied pigeon caught my attention. It was lazily shifting back and forth on its leathery, red feet, while standing in a small puddle which reflected the bright glare of the sun. Repeating a new name—*"I am the one who steps around in the puddle"*—I walked toward the train. With a feeling of "deep moral satisfaction," I saw that there was no blockade on the platform and no ticket inspectors anywhere. The train was almost empty, even though there was not a free inch of space anywhere else in the depot.

Moving down the platform, I caught myself thinking: "And what if a conductor comes later, when I'm already on the train? It's so hard to get everything right!" Without delay I started working on these rising doubts. My glance fell on a sparrow perched on a tree branch, which was spreading out its feathers and energetically shaking itself. I became *"the one who ruffles its feathers."*

There were only two passengers in the railroad car. I moved toward the middle and sat down next to the window. Then suddenly, a miracle! On the floor under the seat opposite me was a large golden coin. I knew immediately that it was meant for me. It certainly was no accident that I'd chosen that exact seat in a virtually empty railroad car! Bending down, I picked it up off the floor. As it turned out, it wasn't a coin at all, but a medal with a profile of Stalin and an inscription along the edge: *"Our cause is just, and we have prevailed!"* The meaning of the message made me laugh—all my doubts are in vain! I am a magician, the creator of my universe.

I smiled broadly, holding the medal in my hand, enjoying the pleasant heaviness of the brass. It shone brightly in the slanting evening sun, shimmering rich yellow with subtle hints of green. Suddenly, by association, a similar sunny day floated up from the depths of my memory. I was seven years old, a sturdy kid with sun-bleached hair, unable to believe my happiness as I clenched a heavy, round object in my hand—an anniversary ruble coin. Just a few moments before, I had been hurrying home to fill up my prize water pistol, when I suddenly noticed something sparkling on the pavement. Now I felt like the possessor of incalculable wealth—this would buy ten (!) whole milkshakes. Irrepressible joy filled me to the brim, wholly and completely. Such an overwhelming feeling of celebration—the discovery of something brand new—usually only occurs in childhood.

Lulled by the moving train, I experienced that extraordinary state of being as I clutched the medal in my hand. As kids, we have all had similar feelings of newness and jubilation. Perhaps my account will help you too remember one of these moments of rapture in your life.

I continued admiring the medal ecstatically. On the backside was written the inscription: "For victory over Germany in World War II, 1941-1945." The face side was worn down and scratched; evidently, the owner of the medal wore it often. Most likely he was now dismayed by his loss, but I, being a good magician, could fully compensate him. A portly man stepped into the car, pleasurably biting off a large piece from a chocolate Eskimo Pie. The renaming was accomplished: *"I am the one who gobbles down the Eskimo pie with pleasure."* I repeated this magical name of the medal's owner and could feel his satisfaction; everything was in order.

The wheels of the train knocked rhythmically, and I recalled my recent doubts with a healthy dose of irony. Truly, *"Our cause is just, and we have prevailed!"*

A few stops later, a middle-aged woman walked in looking very angry. Bent over double, she was carrying an unbelievably huge, heavy handbag. The contents inside were clinking loudly. Coming up alongside me, she stopped, dropped her handbag onto the floor, and noisily plopped down onto the seat next to me, mumbling tiredly: "Whew! What a nightmare!" I could see numerous vodka bottles thrown randomly into the handbag. She was obviously depressed and needed to be renamed. But the sheer volume of the contents of the handbag bewildered me, and I couldn't stop thinking: "Wow! Our people really know how to party big time!"

I was pulled out of this bewildered state when the woman asked me: "Do you happen to know what time it is?" I looked down at my watch and, turning to her, answered: "Quarter past six." She graciously nodded at my reply. So, here was the support signal: *"I am the one who nods my head."* Repeating this name to myself while slightly nodding my head, I watched my neighbor out of the corner of my eye. Gradually, her aggravation and exhaustion left her, she softened noticeably, and her face became smoother.

At the next stop, an old woman came in with her grandson, a fidgety kid of about six, and they sat down opposite us. He was wearing colorful overalls and a stylish cap with a bill almost as long as he was tall. I noticed with satisfaction the result of renaming—the complete transformation of my neighbor from a severe, scowling wench into a relaxed, cheerful woman. Catching sight of the boy, she smiled at him broadly; even her freckles came to life. *"Our cause is just, and we have prevailed!"*

An hour later, my wife and I were walking to the produce market. In front of a seventeen-story building, we witnessed a truly acrobatic feat. An unkempt, old drunk who could barely stand up was attempting a nosedive onto a rough wooden bench. For a long time he took aim, slowly turning around, until finally he dived down headfirst. The bench was indeed on the trajectory of his flight, but his center of gravity had already been transferred to the far side of it. In the end, the fellow performed an elaborate, twisting somersault, rolled over the bench, and landed headfirst onto the ground—all in slow motion. He wriggled around and mumbled incoherently, probably something about his unfortunate landing.

My wife gasped in fright at this spectacle. I, on the other hand, was somewhat impressed by his pirouette and glanced around in search of a support signal. My attention was immediately caught by a candy wrapper kicked up by a gust of wind and sent flying down the road. I happily renamed myself as *"the one who wrappers in the wind!"* My wife started laughing as she shook her head.

Immediately afterwards, we came upon yet another person who was thoroughly celebrating Victory Day. He was moving straight towards us in a wide, sweeping curve, with arms outstretched as if hoping to draw everyone into his embrace. We didn't particularly want to be embraced by this man, though, and stepped to the side. A long-haired fellow on roller blades with orange wheels, who had just purchased a Coke at a kiosk, became the prototype for renaming. *"I am the one who drinks Coca-Cola on rollerblades."* Glancing back, I noticed that the drunken fellow had stopped short, lowering his arms as if suddenly remembering something important.

At that point I remembered the woman I had seen earlier that day with the huge handbag full of vodka and my amazement at the scale of drunkenness in Russia. I realized how commonplace materialization really is in this world. As it turned out, the rollerblades and Coca-Cola did the trick, and we no longer came across any more drunks, although these kinds of marketplaces are usually very seedy.

The medal now hangs in a place of honor. If any doubts about the success of magical "ceremonies" ever come to haunt me, I have only to recall the universal name engraved on that medal: *"Our cause is just, and we have prevailed!"*

Operation "Tractor Drivers"

To use the stale smell of alcohol on the breath to do good—this is also science. For instance, from ten sailors you could collect a gas balloon of stale alcohol breath and take it to the cancer ward of a hospital. Cancer loves to have a drink and would wither away from the alcohol breath. In the country we fumigate potatoes for Colorado beetles with alcohol breath... They lay a couple of guys down in the potatoes and with stakes roll them across the field. They spew out obscenities—and the alcohol breath is spread around properly.

Yuri Koval—*Suer-Vyer*

Three magicians—Papa, Andriukha, and I (Beard)—set out in the beginning of September on a kayak trip along the Kubena River, which flows in the northern part of the Vologda Province. Our trip was nearly finished; all items on the program had been completed: mushroom hunting, a sauna in the woods, fishing, and so on. The weather had been sunny for the entire time. There were no unfavorable signals anywhere, except maybe that at times we had to rename Andriukha, who was constantly amusing us with tales drawn from his rich experiences while kayaking—like how in 1987 a fellow capsized his kayak in the Transpolar Urals, or when the natives from a nearby village stole his ax and handsaw while he was camping overnight.

It was a clear, warm Saturday afternoon, when we arrived at the final point of our itinerary—a small settlement with the beautiful name of Ust-Reka*—and disembarked onto the bank of the Siamzha River where it flowed into the Kubena River. Dragging our boat out of the water to dry, we set up our tent in a small grove and settled down at the edge of the forest next to a campfire. Before long, flaky Vologda potatoes were steaming in our bowls, and we were spooning out globs of fresh, homemade sour cream, which almost resembled butter. As we lounged lazily in the sun after lunch, it suddenly dawned on Andriukha: "Why don't we just leave right now, instead of waiting until tomorrow?"

We had planned to depart at noon the following day on a bus to Vologda (90 miles), and then take the train to Moscow that evening, but we would have to hang around Vologda for half a day. Besides, one more night sleeping in our tent was not particularly attractive to us. Despite warm daytime temperatures, frost was forming at night, and every morning we would find rings of ice floating in the teakettle. Therefore, we had been putting on all our warm clothes during the night, even pulling our knapsacks over us for additional warmth.

Andriukha's proposal, which would allow us to save a day's travel, met with general agreement. By that time, the boat had already dried out, and Papa and Andriukha started packing up our knapsacks while I rushed over to the junction in the road to flag down a passing car. Meanwhile, it was already seven in the evening, and I was beginning to have doubts about the feasibility of the whole undertaking. Just as I arrived at the edge of the dirt road, a car flew past me, leaving behind a cloud of dust which covered the entire area. So I renamed myself as *"the one who raises dust along the road."*

* "Rivermouth." [trans]

The junction of the roads to Vologda, Kharovsk, and Is-tominskaya was not far off—both from our camp and from the outskirts of Ust-Reka. It would be best to go to Kharovsk (25 miles); almost all the trains heading for Moscow stopped there. Over the next forty minutes, two motorcycles sped by, two cars with passengers, and an old, dilapidated tractor. However, I continued *"raising dust along the road."*

Eventually Andriukha came up to me. After waiting there for a while, we decided to set out for the village, intending to make a deal with some local with a motor vehicle for hire. Our situation was made all the more difficult because of our three-seat kayak. Even when taken apart, it was fairly cumbersome and required a roof rack on the car. Before long we came on a brand-new GAZel microbus. But our happiness was premature—first of all, it was nearly out of gas, and second, the dashboard had been pulled out. A short distance farther on the other side of the street, there was a ZIL-157 truck with a bluish cab—also in a state of disrepair. Nearby, a sullen man was rummaging around in an UAZ military jeep. He suspiciously gave us a sidelong glance and grumbled: "That car don't work." After that, we found a red Niva, a white Zhiguli, a Moskvich 412, and several more cars, but by then we'd reached the far side of the village.

Our appearance did not inspire much confidence: Andriukha was wearing a brightly-colored pirate's kerchief on his head, and I was in torn jeans. Andriukha decided to take off his kerchief to make him look less exotic, but that uncovered the upper half of his forehead which shone out as a bright, white stripe in contrast to his well-tanned face.

Based on the research we had conducted, it became clear that drivers in the village of Ust-Reka could be divided into three categories: they were drunk, had just finished taking a sauna, or both. Throughout our investigation we continued vigorously *"raising dust along the road,"* affirming our new name.

The bright red orb of the sun was already hanging low over the forest, tinting the thin veil of clouds and surrounding hills in varied hues of reddish-orange. Our allotment of time was running short; we had one last chance. From the intelligence we'd gathered, we found out that in Ust-Reka there was a two-story building of white brick—a dormitory inhabited primarily by drivers. We walked over to it.

Near the dormitory was a lopsided woodshed, and three men (evidently from the first category) were sitting on the grass sprawled against the wall. As we approached, one of them, wearing a striped sailor's vest draped over his lanky body, lifted his balding, red-haired head and greeted us loudly: "Such people! Mu-u-stached! Be-e-e-arded! What fate has brought you to our tiny village?"

We explained that we were trying to get to Kharovsk, at which point the men, stammering as they hurried to speak, explained that they were the only drivers around. On the plus side, they told us that they had a tractor and would gladly transport us for just three bottles of vodka. Andriukha and I exchanged looks and shook our heads. Riding on a tractor-pulled trailer over a rutted dirt road in the dark—with drivers drunk to the gills—was definitely too risky.

When we tried explaining this, the men lunged to their feet and, repeatedly interrupting each other, assured us that they would deliver us safe and undamaged, if only they could find some diesel. "Striped Vest" was pushing us especially hard.

"What's with you guys? A T-80 is a beast, not a tractor! We'll get you there fast, just like a Mercedes!"

Andriukha answered back that he himself had driven tractors before, and he knew what they'd be getting into. There was no way he would go on such a joyride. The redhead completely lost it, pulling hard at the front of his sweater as if to expose his chest.

"What d'you know?! I've been a tractor driver since birth!"

However, we were as hard as rocks and stood our ground: "We'll only ride in a car, and with a sober driver."

Realizing that the possibility of getting free alcohol was drifting away, the men calmed down, but we could see every possible variant whirling around in their aroused minds. At last, another man of heavier build with dark, straggly hair and a crooked nose suggested: "Well, how about if we go over to Petrov's, on that street over there in the house with the blue porch. He's got a Zhiguli Model 9."

We went over to Petrov's, and his wife opened the door. When she found out the reason for our visit, she sighed in despair: "I'll wake him up, but he probably won't want to go—he's already had a little."

Not long afterwards, shuffling along in felt slippers, Petrov himself appeared on the porch, looking like a huge, good-natured bear. Greedily gulping down a dipper of water, he heard us out, took us over to his car, and guiltily shrugged his shoulders.

"I'd be glad to take you, but it won't work out. Yesterday the boss came over; we went hunting and, well, had a drink as the custom goes. Now I've slept away the whole day, and it would be too much of a bother to drive anywhere after such a good time."

Looking doomed, Petrov advised us to go see Slobodin down the road by the river. As we walked to the other side of the village, Andriukha and I were prepared to just return to our camp. It wouldn't be that big of a deal to hurriedly put up the tent and spend the night. But as long as there remained even the smallest possibility of getting out of there, we felt we had to follow up on it. "There is always a way out," kept passing through my mind, and I continued repeating: *I am the one who raises dust along the road.*

However, we never managed to get to Slobodin's. Not far from the dormitory, we heard "Striped Vest" and "Disheveled" yelling at us: "Hey, guys, come over here!"

Their shouts were insistent, so we came closer. In agitation Striped Vest incoherently explained to us: "Let's go, guys! Kolian is coming! Driving what?! He's got a UAZ military jeep. Who? Kolian? No, Kolian's as sober as a judge. He's coming. Who's Kolian? He drove out to the fields to pick up some folks. Don't worry, he'll be quick! That's his house there, Kolian's, he lives there! Wherever he's gone off to, he'll come back here."

Then an invitation followed to stop in at Striped Vest's place to drink some tea while we waited for Kolian. We had the vague suspicion that the tea party could easily turn into a real party, and then we wouldn't feel like going anywhere; so we flatly refused his proposal. But Striped Vest and Disheveled didn't back down one bit.

"He'll be quick. Kolian's coming back from the field. Where else would he go? He parks the UAZ there at his place. That's the house where Kolian lives."

A couple minute later, we could hear the sound of an engine approaching. The two men boisterously started shouting: "Look! He's coming! Kolian!

At that moment a UAZ came into view, but just before reaching us it swerved around and drove back the other way. Waving their arms and hurling some choice obscenities, the two men rushed after it but were too late. Andriukha and I had our doubts: Was it time to head back to the grove? But Striped Vest seized the initiative. He dragged us off to the edge of the village, ignoring all questions about the advisability of such a maneuver.

"Follow me! We'll find Kolian! C'mon, over there!"

We never did get any kind of reasonable explanation as to why we actually should go "over there." We just shrugged our shoulders and followed after him, *raising dust along the road."*

Soon we came to a hillside, where three small roads joined together. Striped Vest declared: "Well, anyway, Kolian will definitely come by here."*

Meanwhile, the sun had sunk below the horizon, and it was growing dark. An amazing view of the surrounding fields and woodlands opened up before us, and the slender crescent of the new moon floated luminously in the sky. As we contemplated this remarkable scene, Disheveled, who had disappeared earlier chasing after the UAZ, suddenly emerged out of the brush. He lacked the crucial information clarifying the whereabouts of the elusive Kolian.

Right then our attention was attracted by movement at the foot of the hill.

"Kolian is coming!" the men exclaimed in unison.

Yes, it was indeed the dark green UAZ-469, affectionately nicknamed among the people as "the goat," and it was heading straight for us. Striped Vest leaped into the middle of the road, spread his legs out wide, and threw up his hands. The UAZ didn't reduce its speed at all until suddenly it screeched to a halt just a couple feet in front of us, raising a large cloud of dust. Striped Vest and Disheveled climbed into the cabin—obviously, negotiations were being conducted in strict confidentiality. Kolian was looking very severe (evidently

---

* The entire monologue of the Ust-Reka tractor drivers has been significantly abridged due to the profusion of expletives.

he was sober), and judging by his gestures, Striped Vest was using all the power of his oratory skill. Finally, it came to light that Kolian was almost out of gas, and so we were offered an alternative option: to go to Mikhailovskoe (about 12 miles away), and pass the baton on to one of the locals there. That option was cut short by our firm refusal.

Still Striped Vest wouldn't give an inch: "Then we'll just have to fuel up."

We drove up to the woodshed mentioned earlier. Disheveled ran off somewhere, and brought back two polyethylene bottles and a round one-gallon canister of gas and poured them into the tank. It was already almost dark, and we sped off towards the bridge over the Siamzha River, where we could see Papa's ruffled head sticking up out of the bushes.

Left all alone, Papa had put on a warm jacket and set off to admire the sunset from the bridge over the Siamzha. It was high above the river, and a wide panorama of most amazing beauty could be seen from it. On one side, the reddish-orange sun was fading in the cloudless western sky, and on the other, faint yet relentlessly approaching purplish clouds with hints of sinister maroon heralded the coming cold night. To the left, the new moon was rising over the village, and to the right were the dim silhouettes of a few houses scattered across on the hillside. Fog was creeping in over the meadows, and the sky seemed stunningly close to the earth. In the distance the monotonous murmur of water rippling over rapids was heard, broken occasionally by the loud splash of a leaping fish. Papa felt at one with all of nature, merging with it, and this brought a feeling of extraordinary strength and peaceful joy.

Out of the corner of his eye, Papa noticed some sort of dark spot. He didn't try to make out what it was, but on the contrary unfocused his gaze. Then the grass around the dark spot unexpectedly changed into an emerald-green, diamond-shaped ornament which Papa contemplated for a long time. Next the spot turned into a black cat, and the ornament became ordinary dry grasslands dotted with a few small shrubs. Papa had refocused his gaze. The cat was sitting as still as a sculpture. Papa felt that an invisible yet strong thread was connecting him to the cat. He could see that the cat was hunting for field mice. Suddenly it leapt up abruptly and hid in the bushes. Papa's connection with the cat was severed.

The sun had already set, and Papa felt a slight chill. Thoughts crept into his mind: "Where are Andriukha and Beard? Will they really be able to find a car in this backwater village to drive us to town on a Saturday evening? And if they can't find a car, then we'll have to set up the tent in the dark and dump all our gear back out of our knapsacks in lantern light. And sleep in the cold again! And for what?!"

Papa suddenly remembered that just moments before he had been feeling an extraordinary strength within him. There were many names he could choose from, but he settled on one which was unpretentiously elegant: *"I am the one who hunts mice in the meadow."*

In order to warm up, Papa strolled over to the intersection, periodically uttering his new name out loud. Returning, Papa knew that the night would again be cold—probably in the 20's. He could already see his breath. He was tempted to start a large campfire, so that the scouts could cozy up to it when they returned. These alluring thoughts were immediately brushed away. There could be no retreat—the game must be played to the very end. And if they hadn't come back yet, it meant that there was still some hope of leaving.

Papa walked over to the place where he had been observing the cat and saw that it was gracefully creeping towards the bridge. It slipped quietly past Papa, crossed the bridge to the other side of the river, and disappeared. That was an auspicious sign. Right then Papa thought that he could make out in the distance an extravagant "Antelope Gnu" rattletrap filled with a raucous crew coming towards him. A few minutes later the UAZ jeep turned onto the bridge.

In a matter of seconds knapsacks, kayak, and magicians— as well as Striped Vest and Disheveled (probably for supervision over the whole operation)—were loaded into the jeep. Striped Vest, sitting in the front seat, soon dozed off, his head waggling from side to side—the spiritual effort expended in implementing the Great Mission had evidently taken its toll. Kolian drove quickly yet carefully, not speaking a single word for the entire trip, and thirty-five minutes later we arrived at the Kharovsk train station. Kolian's severe face softened only at that moment of triumph when we handed him the "Northern Star"—a bottle of Vologda vodka—and the monetary equivalent of two more bottles, in accordance with the terms we had agreed to. Incidentally, the "Northern Star" was one of two bottles of vodka which we had originally purchased on our trip to trade for fish—the first had been bartered for a medium-sized pike and several perch.

Many times we had wondered: "Why aren't we finding any vodka-lovers to trade with? And what should we do with the other bottle? Don't tell us we'll have to take it back to Moscow!"

But now everything was clear—the second bottle of "Northern Star" had been destined for Kolian.

When we stepped into the brightly lit hall of the station and finally got a good look at each other, we burst out laughing. A thick, gray layer of dust from the road covered us from head to foot, and our knapsacks, too.

Hearing the name Beard had used, Papa uttered: "All the world is the projection of our internal movies. Because you were so impressed by the dust of that passing car, you can see how it materialized."

About an hour later, we were jostling along on the "Severodvinsk – Moscow" train, sorting through the details of our successful departure from that tiny Vologda village with the beautiful name of Ust-Reka.

Forest Gatherings

I like spacetime even though it isn't real.
Richard Bach—*Running from Safety*

Down in the Woods

I met Antonina at the winter ice hole in Moscow. I had already had my swim, and the pleasant coolness had disposed me to conversation. I was discussing Satprem's book *Sri Aurobindo or The Journey of the Consciousness* with this older fellow whom I knew slightly. Then, out of the blue, a small, slight woman interrupted us while drying off after her icy bath: "You know, yesterday I very nearly took off flying. I think today I just might make it."

We introduced ourselves, and I learned that Antonina was passing through the second step of transcendental meditation of the Maharishi. Antonina, a mother of four grown sons, was remarkable for her extraordinary vitality—she bathed in the ice hole, fasted, went to classes at Antonov's Yoga school, sang in a choir, and so on. Extremely talkative, Antonina was always in the loop of esoteric trends and gossip in Moscow. She played a significant role in my life, because that summer she convinced me to go to a gathering sponsored by Club Cosmos—a group founded by Yan Ivanovich

Koltunov*—which took place in July near Serpukhov outside of Moscow.

I borrowed a tent, pad, and sleeping bag from a friend
and went camping for the first time in my life. A long band
of multi-colored tents stretched along the picturesque river.
There were over a thousand participants at the gathering—
more than a hundred had arrived from the Ukrainian city
of Dnepropetrovsk alone. From early morning until very late
at night, a variety of activities was offered—meditative running, yoga and wushu, herbal medicine, swimming, healing,
cleansing techniques, clairvoyance, and clairaudience. In the
evenings spiritual dances were led, followed by intimate dis-
cussions around the campfire to the strains of guitars lasting
far into the night.

It was at this camp that I found out about the Rainbow
Gatherings which happened every year near Petersburg during the summer solstice. Representatives of various spiritual
movements in Russia and even abroad gathered there—practitioners of yoga and wushu, devotees of Krishna and Vis-
sarion, hippies and followers of Native American traditions,
astrologers and psychologists, practitioners of Holodynamics
and Dianetics, Osho devotees and Buddhists, Christians and
Russian pagans and...

Of course, the following June I set off for "Rainbow." The
weather presented a serious challenge—for three days straight
rain poured down in buckets. The tents of those who came
unprepared, the "novices," were soaked completely through.
Many people didn't have a single dry item left, and it still
kept raining and raining. Before long a significant number of
people had left, and then beautiful weather set in! It was at

* Yan Ivanovich Koltunov (b. 1923)—Russian missile designer and re-
searcher of human physical and psychic abilities. [trans]

this gathering that I met Andriukha, who was passionately promoting magical techniques.

Over the next year, I continued my study of magic and by the next gathering felt ready to work with the weather, hoping to avoid a deluge like before. At the same time, I conjured up the participation of many interesting people, much joy, etc. So when my son and I returned home after the gathering, my wife was astounded. We were all suntanned, while in Moscow and Petersburg there had been continual rain with temperatures in the 50's, and at our summerhouse in the country the young seedlings in our garden had all rotted.

Soon afterwards we went to a similar gathering near the Yakhroma River outside of Moscow, and I again made an agreement with the weather. For two weeks we had temperatures in the 80's without any rain at all. When we returned home, we found out that in Moscow and its suburbs it had been cool and rainy.

Forest Sauna

One day while out camping, Andriukha met some military officers who had just completed a boat trip around a lake. They were setting up a sauna in the forest and invited Andriukha to join them. For the benefit of all campers everywhere, we will present here a detailed description of how to build a forest sauna.

First, large stones are stacked into a rock pile. The conical structure must be arranged very carefully, since afterwards this rock pile will be covered over with firewood for a bonfire. The stones are heated to red-hot and can sometimes crack or even shatter into pieces. Therefore, construction of the rock pile must be done with utmost care, so that, even if some of the stones cave in, the pile will remain stable and not tumble down.

When the campfire has burnt down, the coals and ashes are quickly cleared away. Next, an army tent (without the bottom) is set up above the rock pile, and then the sauna is ready. The entrance to the tent must be covered very carefully, and it is best if people enter and exit at the same time, which helps maintain a high temperature in the sauna.

Andriukha thoroughly enjoyed the sauna for about four hours, and the idea occurred to him to construct one like it at the next gathering near Petersburg. But he had to figure out what to use instead of an army tent. He soon devised an alternative design. First, he built a wooden frame, on which several layers of heavy polyethylene plastic were overlapped in lieu of a tent. We had brought large sheets of plastic with us to the camp to cover our tents in the rain.

Three sheets of about ten by sixteen feet work well. If three sauna-lovers each bring one sheet of plastic and some rope, they can enjoy saunas throughout the gathering. It's also good to bring along a good ax, two-handled saw, small shovel, and a pair of heavy gloves.

The frame is made in the following manner: four stakes are driven into the ground so that about three feet remain above the ground, marking the corners of the sauna. A rope is then stretched along the upper perimeter. In this way, we instantly solved several potential problems. First off, a wooden frame would have to be reinforced with nails, which we didn't have. Second, after each sauna a wooden frame would have to be taken apart, since otherwise it would burn up in the next sauna fire—the flames can be rather intense, especially in a strong wind. And third, rope won't poke through the plastic as will the smallest twig on a pole.

Plastic is stretched over the rope frame with the edges held down on the ground by sand. Over time this basic design has undergone numerous improvements. We began to pile up sleeping bags on top of the plastic, lessening the loss of heat while at the same time plugging holes which inevitably appear. After a sauna the sleeping bags may be damp from condensation but can be quickly dried over the warm stones.

Once I had a thick sheet of polyethylene which I had taken to gatherings for three whole years. This record-holder lasted a full twenty-five saunas! If you lay sleeping bags on top, you'll have to reinforce the frame with two poles attached to the tops of diametrically opposite stakes.

Another improvement is to dig a pit in the middle one or two feet deep and about four feet in diameter. Build the rock pile in the center of the pit. Then light several small campfires around its perimeter to which thicker and thicker firewood is gradually added. Fairly quickly the smaller campfires unite into one huge, raging fire, somewhat resembling an ancient furnace used to melt metal.

This works well because the walls of the pit keep the burning firewood from rolling off the rock pile and, what's more, during the sauna you can sit at the edge of the pit, putting your feet down into it. This allows more people to fit into the sauna. The ground on the bottom and sides of the pit can become extremely hot, so much that, if you splash water over them, the water will boil up instantly. Therefore, you should cave in the sides of the pit with a shovel all the way to the bottom and then sprinkle them with wet sand. This sand will become very hot, and you can spread it around the edge of the pit where people sit.

This is really all you need to know in order to construct a forest sauna. I would add that it is best to build it on the bank of a river or lake. Imagine the enjoyment you'll feel as you emerge well-steamed from the sauna to dive into the cool water! Also, you can prepare herb tea in the remaining coals, and when you splash some tea onto the hot stones, the entire sauna will be filled with the pungent aroma of wild herbs.

At that gathering outside of Petersburg we became completely enamored with forest saunas. It was easy to set up saunas there. Stones were everywhere, and the forest was chock full of firewood. Two weeks after "Rainbow," we went to a gathering on the Yakhroma River outside of Moscow. Many interesting events were offered, but, having tasted the delights of forest saunas, we started missing them. We agreed that there were two main reasons which made it difficult to construct a sauna at Yakhroma. First of all, where would we find the large number of stones required? And second, several

gatherings had already taken place in the main meadow where
the camp was being held, plus other campers and fishermen
often stayed there as well. So there was also the problem of
firewood.

This tormented us for the first two days, but on the third
day it dawned on us that stones could be found in the river.
And if we walked up the river away from the main meadow, there wouldn't be any problem with firewood either. The
weather was sweltering hot. Andriukha and I explored along
the Yakhroma River looking for an appropriate place. We
wandered about for half an hour, but both banks of the river
were covered with a heavy growth of trees, bushes, and nettles.
Finally we decided to try thanking the spirit of the woods and
offer it gifts. We had not even finished doing this, when we
spied a small clearing with remarkable yellow sand on a low
bank of the river. We could feel large stones under our feet,
which were ideally suited for building the rock pile. Again
thanking the spirit of the woods, we eagerly set to work.

In the immediate vicinity we discovered an endless sup-
ply of dry firewood, and by that evening we were enjoying a
sauna. The place turned out to be extraordinarily beautiful. A
wall of tall grasses, standing higher than a person, grew all
around, as well as thickets of underbrush, ivy, wild currants,
giant burdock and bluebells, and moss-covered tree trunks. It
was like being in a jungle. We could hardly believe that not
so far away loomed a huge, dirty city with large buildings and
people crushed by hosts of psychological problems.

The Gathering Begins

The next gathering near St. Petersburg was going to be held in Karelia on the shore of Lake Vuoksa. It wasn't called "Rainbow" any more but rather "Summer Solstice Gathering," since the composition of participants had changed. The organizers decided to protect this great sacrament from the harmful influence of marijuana, and therefore the hippies did not participate in the gathering. They conducted their own "Rainbow" outside of Bologoe, in a place which could only be reached by railway handcar. The Indians* mostly went to "Rainbow."

By this time Beard, who came to the gathering with Papa and his son Nikita, had been "converted" to magic. We were accustomed to catching car rides to gatherings and so were not surprised to see two automobiles waiting for us at the "Losevo" railroad platform.

A half hour later we were on a dirt road walking through a forest. As we tramped along the trail to the designated site, being experienced sauna-lovers, we surveyed the surrounding area in search of stones and dry wood. The further we walked, the more confused we became. Where were the boulders and deadwood, so typical of the forests in the Leningrad Region? Along the entire path to the gathering, we didn't come across a single stone, not even one the size of a fist. As for dry conifers, we noticed only a few huge ones, which could only be

---

* Russians who practice Native American traditions. [trans]

cut down with a chainsaw. So we renamed ourselves. Beard, hearing a woodpecker, became *"the one who pecks at the tree,"* and Papa, noticing a sprawling juniper bush—*"the one who twists its branches in fantastic ways."*

After a while we came out onto a large sandy clearing, where several brightly colored tents and a single lone tipi had been set up.* We could tell that this was the main clearing for the gathering. To the north was a pine forest, and to the south—an arm of Lake Vuoksa. This arm looked more like a wide river and was about a quarter mile to the far shore. The marshy bank of the lake was overgrown with tall grasses, which were more like reeds with thick hollow stems. These reeds covered a wide swath of ground along the bank extending westward to the horizon.

We had intentionally arrived a day before the official beginning of the gathering in order to stake out an area for our minicamp which was unthinkable without a sauna. It was essential that the site have convenient access to water, firewood, and suitable stones, and, ideally, that it be in a place difficult to find. We didn't want to go westward into the thick growth of reeds, so we walked along the lake to the east, where we noticed a sandbar along the shore. A person with keen hearing could make out the tapping of a woodpecker drifting up from the twisted growth of reeds. About three hundred yards farther, we noticed a suitable boulder in the water, and next to it—another four stones! This was an auspicious sign, which suggested that it was now time to search for a secluded spot for our tents. Almost immediately we came upon a small meadow in a narrow strip of forest along the shore, surrounded by a dense growth of trees and underbrush.

---

* A traditional Native American dwelling (for more details, see chapter "Chinchinata").

To get back to our knapsacks, we didn't go the way we'd come along the shore, but rather on a path we found through the woods. A surprise was awaiting us. Along the path we saw a large pile of firewood, the size of a good-sized shed, covered with polyethylene plastic held down at the bottom by the exact kind of stones we needed. Then deeper in the pine forest we found an entire residential complex. The woodwork there was especially amazing: sheds nailed together from construction timber, tables which would seat a company of soldiers, posts sunk into the ground on which wooden dishes hung like garlands, sitting logs, "thrones," chairs, benches, and other contrivances, whose purpose we could not even fathom. It felt like we had wandered into a fairytale.

The greatest pleasure, especially for Nikita, was elicited by three objects: a greenhouse, a workout room, and a shower stall, which consisted of a frame of pine poles covered with plastic with a similar door. Upside down plastic jugs, with their bottoms cut off and filled with water, were mounted above the stall. The operating principle of the shower was simple and ingenious: you just unscrewed the plug of one of the bottles and a stream of fresh water would dribble out onto the weary summer visitor. It's true that we did not entirely understand the necessity of this structure, since all of thirty yards away was a splendid, sandy beach, gently washed by the waves of Lake Vuoksa. The workout room consisted of wall bars, parallel bars, horizontal bars, and a wooden bench on which a man was exercising—he was lifting, in turns, wooden barbells and dumbbells.

Completing the picture were solid ladders leaning against the trunks of some ancient pines which had their dry lower branches skillfully sawn off. It was truly a testament to human ingenuity—instead of going into the forest for firewood, they made ladders to climb up into the trees.

Scattered among the structures were various pavilions and large, spacious tents covered in plastic, the edges of which were held down by rows of "sauna" stones. Cars were parked in front of several of the tents. There was no doubt that the settlement had been established many years ago. It made you wonder why this "dacha settlement" was not surrounded by a deep ditch and pointed wooden pickets. Incidentally, the compound was guarded by dogs who immediately started barking maliciously at us. A German Shepherd, tugging on its chain, looked especially threatening. As you may have guessed, the barking dogs definitely needed renaming. For Beard the support signal was an airplane flying over us, and for Papa it was a moth circling over a bush. We acquired the names: *"I am the one who drones in the heavens"* and *"I am the one who circles the bush."*

Returning to our campsite, we took a swim, decided on a spot for the sauna, and hauled over the stones we had previously spotted. We were just setting up the tents, when we were interrupted by an emissary from the dacha settlement.

"Was that that your child teasing my dog, throwing pine cones at it?" the energetic elderly woman exclaimed indignantly.

Without doubt, it sounded a lot like Nikita. We assured her that we would take appropriate measures, but, as it turned out, the real mission of this emissary was something else completely.

The woman, looking us straight in the eyes, anxiously told us: "You have chosen a terrible place to camp—these bushes are full of horse flies and mosquitoes, my dogs will disturb your sleep with their loud barking, and this weekend a noisy crowd of friends and relatives will be coming to visit us."

Guessing the real goal of her visit, we courteously informed her that "mosquitoes don't bother us, and by the time we go to sleep, the dogs and the noisy crowd will already be on their twenty-seventh dream."

Surprised by our audacity, the emissary became nervous and betrayed the real purpose of her visit: "You should find a better place! You will only bother us here and aggravate my dogs."

As the woman spoke, we were still internally droning in the heavens and circling above the bush, and when she finished, we promised to make friends with the dogs. The emissary went back home without achieving anything for her effort.

Gulping down a quick cup of tea and some sandwiches, we set out to look for firewood. Complaining about the foolishness of organizers for choosing such an unfortunate place, we started diligently "pecking at trees" and "twisting the branches." Penetrating deeper into the forest and not finding a single "sauna" stone, we finally reached an area untouched by the summer tourists—all around there were dry, medium-sized pine trees, enough for a hundred saunas.

"It could not have been otherwise, for magicians cannot be without a sauna!" we thought to ourselves.

Eagerly getting down to business, we made several trips and provisioned ourselves with firewood for half the gathering, dragging over nearly a dozen good pine trees. While engaged in this task, we bumped into an old friend who helped us search for the stones we still needed. He showed us an old dugout left over from the war, and in it were four heavy boulders.

The following day we realized that we had overdone it in getting the sauna ready—our bodies ached horribly. Our shoulders were especially painful from carrying our heavy knapsacks and the logs. But all this was forgotten when the canopy door of the sauna swung closed behind us, and we relaxed blissfully near the red-hot stones—after all, we had awaited this moment for an entire year.

After the sauna we had a quick bite to eat and set out for the dances. When we spotted the enormous woodpile near the compound, we started intoning our "dacha" names. The results manifested immediately—there was no one at the compound, and the German Shepherd was sleeping peacefully sprawled on the sand with a pine cone stuck to its front paw. The scene was completely harmonious (reflecting our state after the sauna), and we included this obvious support signal into a new formula for soaring: *"I am the one who lounges around with a pine cone in my paw."*

After the dances, we returned past the "dacha people", sauntering lazily along. We could hear the German Shepherd owner grumbling sullenly: "Look at those vagabonds! They're probably so drunk they can hardly walk. Why are they still sticking around here? They only rile up the dogs."

This made us wonder what our unhappy hostess might have said if we were passing by with quick steps. And we pronounced together: *"I am the one who lounges around with a pine cone in my paw."*

The following day, when we passed by the settlement, the German Shepherd, roaming freely about the clearing, ran up to us and licked Nikita's hands. Its owner ostentatiously turned away. We saw that act as an agreement "signed and sealed" for our peaceful coexistence.

The Arrival of Andriukha

On the following day, the sauna director arrived—Andri-ukha. We met him while wandering around the central clearing. At first we didn't even recognize him, since Andriukha's outfit at the previous gathering had been washed-out clothes made from orange parachute silk. This time, though, he was in shorts, camouflage jacket, cape, and stylish sunglasses. We gave him directions to our campsite, and then continued our exploration to find our old friends.

Each year Andriukha would amaze us at this gathering. Previously, his unusually powerful creativity had manifested in improvements in the design of the sauna. Andriukha had once brought several thick rods of rebar weighing nearly ten pounds, carrying them in his knapsack six miles through eighty-six degree heat. His premise was that by heating the stones from the bottom they could be made even hotter. The inventor dug out a pit, laid stones around the rim, and built a rebar grate on top of them. This served as a foundation for the rock pile. Then firewood was laid under the grate, allowing the stones to be heated from below. The design turned out to be ineffective, and we all breathed a sigh of relief—we did not want to carry metal rods with us to every gathering.*

---

* Papa and Beard do pack in a large metal bucket with the bottom removed, so that food can be cooked very quickly with minimal use of firewood.

Another time Andriukha was inspired by a dugout which two ingenious campers had made at a gathering. Instead of hauling a tent to the camp, they dug a deep trench, laid poles over the top, covered them with fir branches, laid plastic over that, and topped it off with sod. After examining this structure, Andriukha could find no peace—he became obsessed with the idea of building a dugout sauna. His idea has not yet been put into action, but every year he fleshes it out with additional details.

Many times, however, Andriukha's proposals for improvement were actually very sensible. The pinnacle of his creativity was a sauna cover in the form of a tent sewn from parachute cloth with no bottom. The cover fulfilled two functions: to provide added thermal insulation, and to keep the layers of plastic from melting together. This innovation turned out to be almost too successful—it was impossible to sit in the sauna for more than a few minutes, and we had to open up the plastic at the entrance to release some heat!

This year Andriukha's creative impulse took shape in the inscription "BOJ!"* which had been written in indelible ink on a strip of light-colored cloth. When we returned from our walk, this slogan so dear to our hearts stood out above the narrow passage through the thick undergrowth leading to the magician's camp. The artist himself was rocking steadily in his hammock which was skillfully hung between two trees.

Nodding in the direction of the pine logs, he grunted approvingly: "I see you haven't wasted any time." He then told us that on the train from Moscow to St. Petersburg, loud voices during the night had woken him up. It turned out that

---

* BOJ is an abbreviation of the phrase "Bug off, jerk!" This ancient and powerful phrase can be utilized to radically change one's worldview.

there had been an accident on the Oktiabrskaya rail line, and all trains were stopped. The passengers were standing around, excitedly discussing what to do next.

Having an active disposition, Andriukha could not bear to just sit there and wait until the trains started running again. He was a very experienced traveler. Having conquered tall mountain peaks, kayaked down wild rivers, and hiked through taiga, tundra, and deserts, Andriukha had managed to make his way through some of the most remote places of the former Soviet Union. He had a habit of taking the unbeaten path, even when there was obviously a more direct route. Some people thought that Andriukha purposely "cancelled" trains and buses, so that he could get to his destination by some alternate means. As a rule, meeting Andriukha at a gathering began with an impassioned tale about the obstacles which had arisen in his path, and how he had ingeniously overcome them.

For example, most of the participants come to the Yakhroma gathering by commuter train, then on the local bus and, finally, on foot for two miles. Once Andriukha rode to the gathering on a bicycle, proudly explaining to us that he hadn't wanted to depend on the bus schedule nor carry a heavy knapsack. During the gathering Andriukha had to take a trip to Moscow for a doctor's appointment, and he figured that a bicycle would make the trip easier. When he returned from Moscow, he was all scratched up with deep cuts along his right arm and side. We promptly renamed him.

Greedily gulping down some fruit tea right out of the pot, Andriukha, clutching at his breast, told us in a hoarse voice about his adventures. The trip to Moscow began with an unbelievable race on the bicycle, since Andriukha had overslept that morning and was sure he was late for the train. When he stormed into the village, he could hear the rumbling of the train close behind him. The platform was about six hundred yards away along a muddy road which passed around some vegetable gardens. The desperate rider yelled out as loud as he could: "Stepanych,* help me!" Right then he noticed a dry path between the gardens, leading straight to the platform. Reaching the train at the very last moment, Andriukha managed to leap through the door and made it to his appointment at the polyclinic on time.

Previous blood work had shown inflammation in the sauna director's organism. But this time his blood tested perfect by all measures. Dumbfounded, the doctors could only shrug their shoulders and close his case. Overjoyed, Andriukha headed back to the gathering the following day, when he found himself in a bind yet again.

His misfortune began when they cancelled the last long-distance commuter train before a long break in the schedule. You can guess that Andriukha had no intention of waiting four hours in the train depot. Not giving the obstacle any attention, he pushed on with a renewed burst of energy. Riding another train for twelve miles to the train stop closest to our camp, he chose an elaborate route through villages with amusing names like Kuziaevo, Svistukha, and Shustrikovo.** Andriukha planned to conquer the remaining twenty-five miles by bicycle.

As he sped quickly along the polluted highway, his lungs "caught fire," and then his heart started having pains. At one

---

* Magicians sometimes respectfully refer to the Creator as "Stepanych."

** The names of the villages derive from the words *Kuzia* (masculine name, including that of a hobgoblin from a famous cartoon), *svist* (whistle), and *shustro* (quick). [trans]

point he reached a place where he had to risk descending a steep mountainside. Losing control of his bike, he flew head-first over the handlebars.

He managed to recover that evening after a hot sauna, when, stretching out blissfully, he uttered: "Listen... I'm in deep nothingness!"

This is the story we remembered when we heard the sauna director's account of how he had made his way to the gathering along a circuitous route hitchhiking and riding on local buses and commuter trains. And there he was in the hammock. As it turned out, we had managed to slip past Bologoe on the train half an hour before the train accident. We re-named Andriukha as soon as he began his story. We all ended up giving him the same name: *"I am the one who peeps out from under the shorts."* He had left his place in the hammock and was squatting on a small log opposite us in torn shorts with his legs spread wide. Something was peeping out showing that Andriukha belonged to the male gender.

Searching For Stones

As I was lying under the car with oil dripping all over me, the old lady Naina Kievna, suddenly becoming very affectionate and obliging, twice came up wanting me to drive her to Bald Mountain... When the old woman approached me the second time, to end it all with a single stroke, I told her that I'd do it for fifty rubles. At that point she backed off, eyeing me respectfully.

Arkady and Boris Strugatsky—
Monday Starts on Saturday

We cooked up some rice porridge with raisins, figs, dried apricots, and dried bananas for lunch. As we were eating, Natalia, who had taken a sauna with us the day before, walked up to our camp. She was carrying a very heavy stone in her arms. You can imagine that there are always many people who want to take saunas with us. At one gathering Andriukha tried to share his experience in a workshop on how to build a forest sauna. It ended in a complete fiasco—people arrived with their towels, hoping to take a sauna, but after they found out that first they had to haul a lot of stones and firewood, everyone went away. So we decided to start testing people's strength of intention. For the men, we set up this condition: "A ticket into the sauna costs three average-sized pine logs and a stone"; and for the women, they were asked to bring three armloads of kindling, or gather herbs for tea and make a besom.*

Natalia had already "paid" for her ticket far in excess of what was required, so we were surprised to see her carrying a stone. Her need to be active was comparable to Andriukha— she couldn't sit still and so had walked around the entire area in search of stones. Her search was crowned with triumph— she discovered a rich deposit of stones. This pleasant surprise was the result of renaming, since we were regularly "pecking at trees and twisting branches."**

After lunch we set out to check out the deposit. Andriukha remained true to himself, lifting out the heaviest stone and somehow managed to squeeze it into his knapsack.

The line of stone carriers extended for about fifty yards, with Papa at the rear of the procession. At that point a woman named Marianna came rushing towards him across the clearing.

Striding alongside Papa, she tried to catch his attention: "Papa, are you busy now?"

"Can't you see that I'm rolling a heavy stone?"

"Oh, excuse me. I'll try to find you later."

"Sure, you can try."

Papa was quite satisfied with himself—with one short sentence he had avoided being "captured," and at the same time had renamed himself *"the one who is rolling the stone."* He had done this because he knew Marianna too well. After

---

* A bunch of green birch twigs tied together which Russians traditionally use to thrash each other in the sauna to increase blood circulation. [trans]

** Natalia's feats didn't end here. Near the end of the gathering, she found a sizable pile of boulders just forty (!!) yards from our campsite, concealed in the sand at the bottom of a deep hole.

one of their workshops on magic two years before, she had "dumped" a whole slew of her problems on Beard, and he had worked with her several times. But this didn't satisfy Marianna. Whenever she bumped into him, she would keep "flogging" him with the very same problems, not listening to anything he said. Her never-ending attempts to involve Papa were thwarted by his continually passing the buck. "Beard understands your problems better than I do." Last year, just catching sight of Marianna, the magicians would rename themselves together. Her constant onslaught was so crushing that they finally felt compelled to devote an hour and a half to her, and even Papa couldn't weasel out of it.

When Papa had rolled his stone up to their campsite, he did not neglect to share with Beard the happy news. After that, whenever they saw Marianna or her tent, the two comrades-in-arms would "roll stones" in their minds. In this way, Marianna never managed to "latch" onto them during the rest of the gathering. In the spirit of fairness, though, we would note that some of her problems were unexpectedly resolved.

Leasing Out Boulders

Early Sunday morning at camp, Papa set out for his daily ablutions and discovered that the stone pyramid of the rock pile was missing its peak. Papa looked around and noticed a parked car and a tent not far away. Next to them was a substantial fireplace constructed from "our very own" stones.

The water was very shallow for a long stretch near our camp, and while walking through the water to the place where it was deep enough to dive in, our legs would cramp up with the cold. So Papa would simply do three quick push-ups in the water near the shore. We should note that participants at the Petersburg gathering traditionally bathe in the nude, and magicians strictly adhere to this etiquette.*

When Papa emerged from the water, a fat, bearded man in swimming trunks who had stepped out of the tent unexpectedly called out to him: "Hey, you there! Put on your swimming suit—there are women here."

Remembering that he was a magician, Papa decided not to exacerbate the situation. To demand his rights, protesting that we were there first, or to become outraged by the man's pilfering of our stones would mean playing into the generally accepted worldview.

Papa decided to retell the situation in "I": "True, what's the point in my swimming naked? I embarrass me. Maybe it's unpleasant for me to look at what dangles down between my

* In Russia, being naked in public is not illegal. [trans]

legs. If truth be told, it's interesting for me to sneak a peek at me, although I pretend that only big boobs interest me."

Out loud Papa promised to bathe in his swimsuit. The aroma of frying meat wafted in on a breeze. Papa figured that they were grilling shish kebabs on the fire and became *"the one who grills shish kebabs."*

Beard came out to bathe in his swimsuit, in his mind dribbling dry wine over a steaming shish kebab. He was moved by the picture which opened before him—the portly man, tenderly pressing a cocker spaniel close to his chest, was carrying it into the deeper water. Gently lowering the dog in, our mustachioed citizen started to play with it, throwing a small rubber ball. They noisily romped around in the water, utterly pleased with each other.

Satisfied with the change, Beard waited until the fat man was walking back to warm up by the fire. Scratching at his beard, he sauntered over to negotiate.

The man greeted him cordially: "We borrowed some stones from you. But don't worry, we're leaving after lunch."

A couple hours later, as Andriukha set out to fetch water for tea, the fat man approached him, holding out two polyethylene bottles of water: "Thanks for the stones. Here's some good Petersburg water! We have a bit of firewood left over, too. Hopefully, it'll come in handy."

The "little bit of firewood" turned out to be three medium-sized pine trees and a large, branchy fir.

Workshop in the Woods

When a person attains success through spiritual or psychological practices, the desire often arises to share his experience with others. We too feel this impulse, and magician's workshops have become as common at gatherings as the spiritual dances and Native American tipis. Nowadays we conduct workshops at gatherings because of so many requests, or simply out of boredom.

At one gathering, we were introducing participants to the technique of renaming. People who lead seminars in esotericism or psychology sometimes encounter "provocateurs" who try to disrupt the class. One such provocateur, Vasya—a gray-haired, middle-aged man with a sparse goatee—appeared at our workshop, hiding in some pine trees behind our backs. When he had first arrived at the main clearing at the beginning of the gathering, he was pulling a two-wheeled cart—the kind Russians are so fond of—loaded down with his knapsack so large as to inspire holy terror.

About halfway through our workshop, he unexpectedly stood up from his camp chair and indignantly announced that magic was all idolatry. We asked Vasya to explain what he meant, as we started repeating in our minds the name: *"I am the one who carries my knapsack on wheels."* He ignored our question and set off on a long tirade, in which he repeated many times words like "understanding" and "mutual respect." We proposed to the participants that we rename this "invader," and amusing names poured out to him from every direction.

241

This only added fuel to his fire, and Vasya appealed to the audience: "You know, these guys are really just mocking us!" His accusations were drowned out by laughter all around.

Finally Vasya, in order to once and for all unmask the idolaters, delivered what he believed to be his coup de grâce: "At the last gathering they gave me a beaded talisman which I wore on my breast for an entire year. But today when I went swimming, I took the talisman off and forgot it there. I returned later and searched for it for a long time, but it was no good. If you are such great magicians, then find my talisman."

Andriukha recommended to Vasya that in order to find his talisman he should repeat the name: *"The winged one above the bald spot."*

In response, Vasya dramatically declared: "What sort of guarantee can you give that if I repeat this gibberish I'll find the talisman?"

"We guarantee that if you don't think about the talisman at all, then you'll find it."

Everyone again burst into laughter. Vasya didn't calm down, though, and we proposed that the audience repeat the name together: *"I am the one who understands and mutually respects Vasya."* This proposal was enthusiastically accepted, and full-voiced mutual respect followed each of Vasya's proclamations. In the end, he was satisfied, having compelled the idolaters to express their understanding to him, and with a look of triumph he abandoned the "podium," taking his camp chair with him.

By this time the number of participants at our seminar had increased noticeably. People began stepping into the circle, talking about their personal issues, after which the audience chose new names for them. One of the first to come in was a nice-looking girl who reported that two days before, her girlfriend's kitty had disappeared. Someone proposed the name: *"I am the one who digs a pinecone with a hole,"* but realizing his mistake, corrected himself: "I am the one who digs a hole with a pinecone." But everyone liked the first name better. The girl started walking around the circle, repeating that she was digging a pinecone with a hole.

Suddenly a longhaired fellow in a striped vest exclaimed: "Is that your kitty over there?" Everyone turned around to look where he was pointing, and the girl dashed off at full speed towards the animal. A minute later she was taking the rascal to task as she swept it up into her arms.

"The magicians arranged this!" a mocking snicker was heard.

"Of course we did!" we confirmed confidently amidst the onslaught of laughter, "and we also arranged the exclamation: 'The magicians arranged this!'"

When the laughter had died down, a fiery brunette stepped into the middle: "I just lost an earring, but I figured that it would be nearly impossible to find it in the sand and pine needles. I was going to announce this when the girl finished talking about the kitty, and told my friend. He renamed me, and almost immediately this person here handed me my earring which she'd found."

"Well, *this* was arranged for sure!" several voices rang out in response.

In the end, we announced that the place where the workshop was being conducted would from then on be a power spot. Consequently, all pinecones located inside the "magical" circle were "energized" and could help resolve many problems. At that point the workshop participants rushed to gather the miraculous pinecones.

The seminar was concluded with a grand parade. Taking hands, we all formed a circle. Each in turn stepped into the circle, repeating their new name, and a powerful choir of voices echoed it back to them. A couple of the names stick in our memory: *"I am the one who pastes fish scales on the table,"* and *"I am the one who hunts the boot with a sporting rifle."*

After the workshop Nikita, all excited, walked up to us and exclaimed: "It turns out that renaming is way easier than giving thanks!"*

That evening a seven-year-old boy, Vanya, told us that he had lost his handmade wooden nunchucks. After noticing how the strong winds fluttered the colorful flags in the clearing, he composed the formula: *"I am the one who flaps in the wind."* The next time we saw Vanya, proudly brandishing his nunchucks, he casually said: "Magic really does work."

The following day we ran into Vasya: "My talisman was found. Actually, I employed three planes of being for this. When I saw some boys swimming where I'd lost it, it flashed into my mind that, if anyone could find my talisman, it's got to be them. So I gave them the mission of finding it. God helped me find it, but I suppose that magic was somewhat to blame as well."

After these cryptic words, Vasya proudly sat down in his camp chair. For a long time afterwards we speculated about what the third plane had been, as well as the "blame" of magic in the whole affair. On the last day of the gathering, Vasya embraced us movingly, handing us each a half-ounce piece of "Fairytales of Pushkin" chocolate.

---

* We remind the reader that in the story "The Cake," Nikita had mentioned this story with the cat as the one which had impressed him the most. In fact, he began regularly using magical techniques right after this event.

How Nikita "Summoned" the Sun

We had beautiful, sunny weather for the first five days of the gathering. But one morning Andriukha woke up earlier than everyone and, looking out of the tent, announced: "Hey, guys, the whole sky is clouded over; a weather front is coming. We might as well leave—that's it for the good weather!"

Later while Beard was swimming, he noticed sporadic circles appearing on the surface of the water—it was beginning to sprinkle.

Beard caught the sound of children's voices in the distance. The kids at the neighboring camp, where an aikido sports school had been established, were enthusiastically scrubbing the outside surface of a huge, sooty cauldron. Beard never ceased to be amazed at this mysterious routine chore three times a day—after all, magicians are so lazy that they rarely even wash the inside of their cooking pot. First off, they don't eat canned meat or fish, mainly porridge; and second, cooking rice, which makes the walls of cooking vessels smooth and lily-white, results in wonderfully clean pots (and dishes).

Beard imagined himself as don Juan, compelling Carlos to eliminate his feelings of self-importance and practice not-doing—to polish his pot mirror-bright. Incidentally, the ingenuity of this renowned Nagual in no way compared to the sophistication of Sergeant Suleimanov, who would ruthlessly torture new military conscripts. Once soon after being drafted into the army, Beard had all but reached enlightenment when he had been assigned to kitchen duty. He had to peel a tub of

potatoes all night long with a homemade "knife." This knife
was actually the handle of an aluminum spoon which Beard
had painstakingly sharpened against a stone. The poignancy
of the situation was all the more heightened by the fact that,
every time Beard came into contact with either the tub or
the water, he received an invigorating electrical shock because
somewhere a wire was ruptured.

A huge, cold drop of rain, slapping Beard on top of his
head, brought him back to reality, and he started searching
for a soaring formula: *"I am the one who sharpens the spoon
against granite," "I am the one who forces little Carlos to scrub the
pot,"* and *"I am the one who scrubs the pot."* Unexpectedly Beard
heard: "C'mon, scrub harder!" This was the children's trainer
approaching, so the final name was chosen. For several days
the magicians would occasionally "scrub the pots," and the
weather front which Andriukha had promised veered off in
another direction.

One night Papa went out of his tent to pee. It was quiet,
and a light rain was sprinkling down. Papa carefully covered
the tent and a good-sized pile of firewood with plastic, holding the edges down with large "sauna" stones.

The next morning the magicians were awoken by drum-
ming—pouring rain was lashing mercilessly against the tent.
Against such raging elements, "scrubbing the pot" seemed
unconvincing—all the more so, because the excited voice of
Andriukha rang out: "Hey, guys, how's it going in your tent?
Is it dry in there?"

"Yeah, everything's good; the bottom is waterproof, and
there's plastic on top."

"Well, I woke up with my sleeping bag completely soaked.
There's a huge puddle inside my tent."

Then we heard some mournful muttering. "JENGARDEN,
JENGARDEN, JENGARDEN..." This was Andriukha

chanting an anti-storm mantra. Beard and Papa joined in with their incantations. Rather quickly the rain let up, and Andriukha and Nikita crawled out of their tents. Andriukha lit a fire and started constructing a frame to dry his stuff on.

Finally, pangs of hunger compelled Papa to crawl out into the big, wide world. He set out to fetch water. On the shore of the lake he came upon a fascinating sight: Nikita—in a yellow rain poncho resembling a wizard's cloak, his eyes shut tightly—was performing a magical dance with wild abandon, spontaneously shouting out any mantra which happened to come to him. Papa decided not to disturb this sacrament and returned to the campsite, remembering that in the folds of the plastic covering the tent he could collect more than a bucket of crystal-clear rainwater.

After breakfast, the rain stopped completely, and we headed for the main camp which was situated in a low-lying area. Arriving, we saw that it had been transformed into a swamp dotted by small lakes with forlorn tents rising up out of them.

Lena walked up to us: "So, what's the deal, magicians. Can't you change the weather?! Everything we have is completely soaked. What should we do? Hang our stuff out to dry? Or will the rain come back?"

"You should've brought plastic with you," muttered Papa under his breath, and then added out loud with confidence: "The sun will come out in half an hour."

Exactly at the appointed time, sunbeams started kindling billions of water drops, emitting a myriad of tiny, glistening rainbows. The birds were chirping deafeningly, and the participants at the gathering, much more cheerful now, hung their wet belongings out to dry.

Returning to our campsite, we saw Nikita swinging in the hammock. A mysteriously meaningful smile played across his face which seemed to say: "I'm the one who really knows why the sun came out!"

Papa crawled into the food tent looking for some nuts and came across a bag he'd completely forgotten about. In it he found the melted chocolate bar which Beard had bought for Nikita at Petersburg Station, as well as a packet of four creamy *Fruttis* yogurts which Nikita's kind mother had given him for the road. Papa triumphantly handed the treats to the hero of the day. The truth of the matter is that Nikita usually ate up all the sweets in the first three days, and then suffered greatly after that, melodramatically bemoaning the lack of treats. The pure, unadulterated delight which appeared on that kid's face when he saw those treats was fixed into a new name: *"I am the one who eats yogurt in the hammock."*

More than once Papa has utilized this name—for instance, when Nikita didn't show up at our camp for two whole days. When he finally appeared, he was half-starved and proclaimed in a pained voice: "I'm never coming to your gatherings again! It's boring here." Incidentally, Papa used two other "powerful" names as well: *"I am the one who summons the sun"* and *"I am the one who is in charge of building the sauna."*

This latter name originated at a time when Nikita was hanging out with a group of folks he knew well from previous gatherings. They were all well-experienced in forest saunas. Their passionate desire to take a sauna was kindled by Nikita's highly-detailed tales of how he would bliss out on the warm sand next to the red-hot stones. Then one day, during evening dances, we heard a sensational report that Nikita had set up an alternate sauna and was its director.

Nikita, in his twelve years, already had extremely rich experience with saunas. In the city Papa would take a sauna every Tuesday, and when his son was five years old, he began bringing him along. Soon the little tyke got to know all the regulars. They were always encouraging Nikita, marveling at his high tolerance for heat. Climbing up onto the highest bench, he could "out-sit" many healthy, robust men, and then bravely leap into the icy pool.

Every June Papa and Nikita would make besoms at their dacha garden—the kid would climb to the top of birch trees which would bend over under his weight, allowing Papa to snip off the long, flexible branches with clippers.

Nikita attended a gathering for the first time when he was eight. The original formation and subsequent rapid development of the forest sauna happened before his very eyes. Furthermore, he always enthusiastically participated in finding and transporting stones, bringing in firewood, arranging the rock pile, and so on. Therefore, we were not surprised that this sixth-grader was now directing big, brawny men in building a sauna, manifesting Andriukha's long-held dream of spreading the use of forest saunas.

When Nikita dropped in on our camp a couple days later, Andriukha said sarcastically: "Do you have a license for this? I bet they sat you down on a stump, covered you in bronze paint, and spoon-fed you condensed milk—that's why you haven't been back for so long!"

But Nikita just smiled wistfully, believing that he truly deserved such honors.

Chinchinata

The Indians always add a special color to gatherings.* Each of them belongs to a specific tribe and clan (Ojibwe, Dakota, Sioux, etc.).

The Indians live in real tipis made from pieces of buckskin stitched together, which are stretched onto a frame of poles about sixteen feet long. The tipi cover is decorated with symbolic designs, bells on the flaps jingle in the wind, and the smoke from the fire inside curls up between the poles. Tipis are one of the few places in the camp where there are no mosquitoes. This is truly a dwelling becoming to a human being in contrast to a cramped tent. Up to twenty people can crowd into a two-person tipi to get out of the rain, or to listen to a mini-concert.

Indians offer rousing concerts of Latin American music using traditional instruments: small guitars, zampoña (bamboo pan pipe), kena (low-toned shepherd's pipe), buckskin-covered tambourine painted with the image of a condor, maracas, and so on.

At this gathering the Indians were represented only by Chief Wapiti (remember that the others had gone to Rainbow that year). He was a stocky, hook-nosed fellow, about thirty-five

---

* The following two paragraphs represent a slightly revised excerpt of an article by Niki Samoshko from the magazine *Rainbow* in 1996. Since we are not versed in the subtleties of Native American ritual, there may be some mistakes and discrepancies in our description.

years old, of average height, with long sideburns and a stern demeanor. He usually wore a black felt hat with feathers fastened to it, worn-out moccasins, a leather vest, and loincloth.

Rumors circulated that Wapiti had once lived in an Ojibwe tribe in Canada and sometimes knew their customs better than the Native Americans themselves. It was also said that he hunted bear alone with only a bear-spear. What's more, Wapiti was a *Fire Tender*—that is, a person sanctioned to communicate with fire. His functions included selecting, heating, and carrying stones to the tipi specially designated for the Native American sweat lodge,* and also lighting the fire with the sun using a lens during opening and closing ceremonies at gatherings.

Following is a detailed description of this ritual. All participants at the gathering formed a huge circle, in the center of which stood the Fire Tender. He was attired in ceremonial clothes consisting of moccasins, pants, a vest worn over his bare chest, and a narrow headband at the top of his forehead. His solemn appearance was completed by a mysterious amulet on his breast and a large knife in a reddish leather sheath on his belt. Everything was covered in artistic colorful designs embroidered with large beads.

Wapiti ignited the main campfire in the central clearing, and from that four other campfires were lit in the four directions. The Chief then picked up a two-foot long, carved wooden pipe and, raising it high into the air on his outstretched arms, he turned towards each of the directions, filling the forest with loud, guttural singing which brought shivers up

---

* The main difference which distinguishes a Native American sweat lodge from a forest sauna is that small stones are heated to red-hot on the campfire and then carried into the tipi by the Fire Tender in a cast iron pan (which Wapiti brought to the gathering especially for this purpose).

everyone's spine. At the close of the ceremony, Wapiti walked around the circle, allowing each person to touch the sacred pipe and to offer a prayer for everyone at the gathering—or the entire Universe—to share impressions about the gathering, or to just be silent.

One wonderful morning, when participants in the Dances of Universal Peace were dancing in a large circle, the Chief stepped into the center with Mamedananda, the dance leader. He was dressed in attire emphasizing the significance of that special moment—a "poncho" made from a blue army blanket with black stripes and bordered with a band of bright crimson material. Mamedananda announced that Wapiti was going to lead a dance from his tribe. The Chief explained that real Native Americans actually perform this dance, insinuating that the Native American dances led by Mamedananda were contrived and had no relation whatsoever to Native Americans.

The circle divided up into partners. The dance was accompanied by singing two words: "Ovodey" and "Chinchinata." First the couples walked forward, holding hands, singing "Ovodey" until the Chief struck a tambourine decorated with a painting of an eagle. Then the couple would turn together while repeating the word "Chinchinata"—completing a full circle with each repetition—until the tambourine again was played. Wapiti loudly chanted the words of the dance. "Ovodey" was sung slowly, and, correspondingly, the dancers were supposed to walk slowly forward. Then "Chinchinata" was sung quickly, and the dance sped up as well, causing a dense cloud of dust to rise up covering the entire clearing. In general, the dance reminded us of alertness drills for nursery school children. A beatific smile spread across Wapiti's face.

When the dance ended, many of the participants all but fell down in laughter, and Mamedananda kept laughing until tears came to his eyes. This was because spiritual dances are generally accompanied by beautiful, harmonious melodies, and the inner rhythm is strictly maintained. And in partner dances, partners are usually changed.

After this dance, magicians gave Wapiti the name CHINCHINATA.

One evening news circulated around the camp that Wapiti had caught a poacher! As it turned out, it was Nikita, who had pruned off some young fir branches with the intention of building a hut.

The Fireman insisted: "This is a precedent! We'll have to set up a court!" At that point Papa recalled that two years ago he had given Chinchinata several stones from our sauna for his "Sweat Lodge." The Chief especially liked crowning the rock pile with round stones. Papa became *"the one who gives a stone to the Fire Tender,"* and in this way Nikita's punishment was limited to a public reprimand.

Several days later, Beard and Papa were occupied with their usual business—leisurely cutting firewood for the sauna which would take place every other day.

Papa mentioned in passing: "It wouldn't hurt to split up the big logs, so they'll burn all the way down."

"And what do you plan to split them with?" the question resounded from the bushes, and Chinchinata emerged into our camp.

"I'm just fantasizing," Papa said casually.

"Have you seen my maul?" the Chief asked, with dignity stroking his rounded belly which peeped out from under his vest. It's been two days since I last saw it."

"We're too lazy to split wood. We just use smaller pines; that way we don't have to use a maul."

"People say that you can help me find it."

"You should repeat: *'I am the one who strokes my belly,'* and it'll show up."

Chinchinata looked at us suspiciously, and, unable to hold back our incisive smiles, we advised him not only to repeat the name, but also to be sure to stroke his belly more often—and definitely always clockwise. Realizing that that was all he was going to get out of us, the Chief went away.

A couple hours later, we set out for the main camp and on the way heard the booming blows of a maul at work.

Retelling in "I"

Cleaning Up

Oh, well, once again I didn't clean up my room today.* Why do I even bother telling me anymore? Dust is strewn all over the floor, but I couldn't care less. See, I just forgot! And why shouldn't *I* forget? Why am I the only one to think about it, while I just laze around doing nothing? I mean, there really was no time during the day for me to sort out the pile of clothes on the chair? And those muddy tennis shoes I wore to the gathering, will they be lying there in the hall forever? And that frying pan for fish which has been there since yesterday, I haven't had time to clean it either?

Well, I realize that I have to sit down and write another book right away; paper is scattered everywhere. Probably, like always, I'm just waiting until I clean it up for me. Of course, I didn't bother to make anything to eat. I boiled potatoes?! Now *that* is some achievement. And don't bother renaming me; I know my monkey business.

Roaches

I walk into the kitchen and lo and behold—I'm scuttling all over the place. I'm everywhere on the table, the walls, and in

---

* The first three stories in this section are narrated by women. [trans]

the sink, so tiny and nimble, with little whiskers sticking out. It makes me sick just to look at me! I creep and I crawl, and there are so many of me—there's no hope! I'm already afraid to even step into the kitchen. I've sprinkled me with powders, set traps for me—nothing seems to affect me. I'm tough!

Then I began to reason with me nicely. I asked me graciously: would it be possible for me to migrate somewhere else? I even gave me a gift, but I cannot read any feelings reflected on my bewhiskered, insolent snout. I creep and I crawl. Maybe I just like frightening me. Probably I want to draw me into total hysterics.

The Green Dragon

"What a scumbag I am! I got sloshed again!"

"What am I yelling at me for? So I got a little drunk; I have every right to."

"How much will I drink? I wonder how I manage to put so much in my body and still have room for more! I don't know what to do with me. Beat me up, or what? Call the police? It's just too much for me…"

"Bug off!"

"How dare I say that! How dare I say 'bug off!' to me. I'm pushing me too hard; I'm just a drunken bitch! Other people are decent folks, but only I get drunk as a pig. Look at me—I can't even stand up. Watch out, dimwit! I'm going to drop my phone on the floor."

"I've had enough of my complaining. I just keep going on and on and on. I'd better give me ten rubles!"

"No way! It's never enough with me; I always need another bottle to suck on. Where else am I off to? And when will I get enough?! I'm sick of me, scumbag!"

"Will I shut up or what?! I'm sick of me, too. I'm puttering around all day, shaking my gray head!"

"I hope I die! Get out of here! Anywhere! And don't come back!"

"Bug off…"

A Scene in a Bus

"Why am I pushing me in the back?"

"I'm not pushing me in the back. I'm just asking: 'Am I getting off at the next stop?'"

"Yes, I am, but, I know, I don't have to push me in the back. That's just rude."

"I know what's rude; so I mean I can't even touch me? Well, OK, but I didn't do it on purpose."

"Well, OK, never mind."

The Vigilent Boss

My boss, Galina Panteleevna, used to unnerve me first thing in the morning. Always keeping an eye on her huge, shiny watch, she would ominously mutter through clenched teeth: "Today you arrived on time." That put me on the edge from the start. The next day she'd note: "Maria, today you were two seconds late." And if I arrived two minutes late, she would raise such a fuss that I'd be shaking all day long. Generally, I'm a calm person, but for me Panteleevna was like a red flag is to a bull.

Waking up I can't get up.
My body's tired, my eyes are blurry.

My comb is lost, and where's my key?
I'm late for work, I have to hurry.

Standing near my office door,
I wait, belligerent, irate,
And staring crossly at the clock,
I mutter peevishly: "Checkmate!"

It's 8:00! Now 8:03!
I'm only scolding me, you see!
But, my friend, why make a scene?
Go to sleep, and I'll kiss me.

Now Panteleevna always relates to me with respect, and I set my alarm fifteen minutes early.

The Commandant

Our work collective finally received payment for a commercial project which we'd long since completed. As the research supervisor, I had the right to dispense these funds, and at a meeting we decided to pay each participant according to his contribution. The head of the department, Anton Polikarpych, had not had much of a role in this work, and his share turned out to be minimal. When he found out about our decision, he flew into a rage and threatened to fire me. This happened on Friday. On Saturday, at a magician's seminar, I retold the dispute in "I."

I decided not to give in to me and to pay me according to my real contribution to the work. I summoned me and delivered my compensation.

After giving me the money and requesting a receipt, I asked me: "But how come I received so little?"

"My work has been properly remunerated according to my participation and position."

I turned crimson and shouted loudly that I would not take this money and would instead dispense the funds myself. After suggesting that I discuss it calmly, I defiantly turned away and announced: "I'm a crook and want to swindle me, so I'm dismissing me from work. I'm the boss here and won't allow me to push me around."

After that I wrote me a report contending that I'm cheating me.

On Monday morning Anton Polikarpych went to complain to upper management, but they wouldn't support him. When he returned to the office, he immediately came up to me and said: "Let's just consider that this never happened."

The Kitchen and the Couch

I'm bustling about the kitchen and hear me jingling the spoons and closing the cabinet doors. I do this carefully while lying on the couch writing my essays; I'm experimenting. Again I start jangling. I'm so restless. How much can I keep jangling things around? It's amazing how loudly I'm clinking now; it's delightful to me.

I quieted down somewhat in the kitchen: have I fallen ill? Exactly. I've fallen ill because I can hear my muffled cough coming from the kitchen. So what does this have to do with the kitchen? Comfortably settled on the couch, I'm writing and don't see what I'm doing in the kitchen. Right then I saw me heading towards the mirror. I combed my hair and quietly disappeared, probably back to the kitchen. What did I find there? I felt myself on the couch and realized where I actually was. On the couch I am active and creative, but in the kitchen it's way too mysterious. I came back from the kitchen and determinedly started turning off the lights in the apartment.

"And where's my book which I gave me to read yesterday?" I asked me. "It's in my bag; I put it in there yesterday and intentionally brought my attention to this. I really don't remember?"

I started rubbing cream on me. Most likely, this is helping me get ready to read the book. Actually, I don't want to read this book at all, but I heard me rustling the pages, and felt me prop my knee against my leg.

I removed my leg and inquired: "Am I bothering me?"

"No!" I cheerfully answered, moving still farther away from me, fervently scribbling with my pen.

Right then I felt how cold my feet were and said to me: "I thought this anemia wasn't a deficiency of blood."

"Bless me, bless me," I answered me. "How can I be anemic on such a marvelous evening?"

Rustling the pages not only by moving the pen but also with the sleeve of my suit, I found myself a name: "I am the swishing rustler." Just then I heard me swishing and rustling along the stairs.

"Up with hips!" I suddenly heard my own joyful exclamation and, scratching my thigh, I consulted me: "What was that?"

"It was such a great moment for scratching," I answered me with laughter and then became silent for a long time.

Outside the window I ride around the streets loudly roaring, despite the fact that I want to sleep. I also rumble along the rails, beating out a rhythm: Like this, and this, and this… Annoyed I go off to drink tea in my kitchen and hear my own yawn coming from the direction of the couch.

"But I don't yawn," I say to me. "It's that I can't see me very well."

Afterword

"If all fixed beliefs are illusions, then even your proposition that all fixed beliefs are illusions is also an illusion."
"That is absolutely true."
"Then what can one believe in?"
"Exactly."

Luke Rhinehart—Transformation

Any theory professing some degree of universality is a myth.

Ernest Tsvetkov—Psychonomics
or the Programmable Mind

Never expect someone else to show you the way or to make you happy.

Richard Bach—Running From Safety

"It is no longer up to you whether to go or not, my dear. You are a myth, a legend; and rumor ascribes to you great deeds."
"Rumor doesn't come up with such foolishness."
"I can't believe that!"
"Yes, Mr. Ramkopf, I demand that you withdraw this ridiculous book."

From the film Münchhausen Himself

We expect that, after reading this book, many readers will immediately begin practicing magical techniques, and we're certain that they will succeed.

If you wish to schedule a training session in your city, please contact us by email at: *g_u_rangov@mail.ru* or *d_o_lohov@aport.ru*; our webpage is *www.simoron.ru*.

You can obtain excellent training online by participating in the Magicians Symposium at *http://www.simoron.ru/ phpBB3/*. Also, in the newsletter "Magical Fireworks" you can find news from magician's conferences, material from seminars, and magical stories. To subscribe, go online to *http:// subscribe.ru/catalog/psychology.wizards.**

The authors *do not maintain an office to receive clients*; however, anyone who wishes to attain mastery in magic can attend their seminars. The authors *do not answer letters* requesting mantras, renaming, etc., but rather encourage the reader *to be creative* and take the initiative to deal with their issues themselves. In order to learn something, you must first have the intention to learn it—i.e., you must start *doing work on your own*. Whoever *attempts* to become a magician surely *becomes* one. "Whether you succeed or not, *just do something, anything*! Don't sit on your hands waiting for someone else to solve your problems."

To be a magician, all you have to do is try applying the techniques in various sequences at every opportunity, carefully cultivating *your personal power*. People often write that small issues are nearly always resolved easily, but with the big ones—nothing. We believe that it is best not to distinguish

---

* The online resources cited here are in the Russian language. [trans]

between important and secondary goals. Don't be upset if you do not get the results you expect, but be encouraged by your achievements, attributing to yourself in advance ever higher standing as a magician. If something does not resolve itself over a long period of time, and you have persistently worked with it creatively, then something unexpected will surely happen instead: if not money, then love; if not love, then health; if not health, then money.

Sometimes we get the question: "I did everything written in the book but still nothing happened. What did I do wrong?"

Keep faith! And remember: *"Everything that I do, I do in the best possible way."*

Many other letters ask: "Which particular technique should I use to resolve an issue?" or "Which technique is the most powerful?" We would respond by stressing that the key element is to remember that *you are a magician* (i.e., you have the power to alter your world), so it's really not relevant which specific technique you use—giving thanks to the obstacle, renaming yourself, or performing a magical dance. It's not the particular technique which is important, but rather the creative impulse behind it, the flight of your imagination—when your eyes are ablaze with light and you experience that sensuous warmth glowing within your heart, that moment when you feel on the verge of taking off into space…

We hope that you will *play* with magic, discovering the joy of practicing magic which is so well expressed in this song of Ostap Bender:

> I do not weep, I do not cry.
> Just ask me, friend, I will not lie.
> All life's a game, and who's to blame?
> I love this life, I'm glad I came!

Why should I apologize?
They just submit, why agonize?
Surely skill and joyous glee
By right must charge a modest fee.

You must agree that such allure—
To hit the mark although obscure,
My eagle-eye, my hustle—and
Forbidden fruit drops in my hand.

What joy to slip along the edge!
Be still, my angels—don't dismay!
Please do not judge me for my sins,
But see how beautifully I play!

Recommended Reading

Russian Folk Tales.

Bach, Richard. *Illusions* (1977). *Running from Safety* (1994).
Bandler, Richard. *Using Your Brain for a Change* (1985).
Brown, Joseph Epes. *The Sacred Pipe* (1953).
Carroll, Lewis. *Alice's Adventures in Wonderland* (1865).
Through the Looking Glass (1871).
Castaneda, Carlos. *The Teachings of Don Juan* (1968). *A Separate Reality* (1971). *Journey to Ixtlan* (1972). *Tales of Power* (1974). *The Second Ring of Power* (1977). *The Eagle's Gift* (1981). *The Fire From Within* (1984). *The Power of Silence* (1987). *The Art of Dreaming* (1993).
Chopra, Deepak. *The Way of the Wizard* (1995).
Coelho, Paulo. *The Alchemist* (1988). *The Fifth Mountain* (1996). *Veronica Decides to Die* (1998). *The Devil and Miss Prym* (2000).
Donner, Florinda. *Being-in-Dreaming* (1991).
Fry, Max. *Nest of the Chimera. My Ragnarok* (1998).
Garfield, Patricia. *Creative Dreaming* (1974).
Harner, Michael. *The Way of the Shaman* (1980).
Heinlein, Robert. *Stranger in a Strange Land* (1961).
King, Serge. *Urban Shaman* (1990).
Kliuev, Evgeny. *Between Two Chairs* (1988). *Book of Ghosts* (2001).
Koval, Yuri. *The Lightest Boat in the World* (1984). *Syer-Vyer* (1998).

265

LaBerge, Stephen. *Lucid Dreaming* (1985). *Lucid Dreaming: A Concise Guide to Awakening in Your Dreams and in Your Life* (2004).

Le Guin, Ursula. *A Wizard of Earthsea* (1968).

Lukyanenko, Sergey. *Labyrinth of Reflections* (1997). *False Mirrors* (1999).

Monroe, Robert. *Journeys out of the Body* (1971). *Far Journeys* (1992). *Ultimate Journey* (1994).

Neihardt, John. *Black Elk Speaks* (1932).

Nosov, Nikolay. *The Adventures of Neznaika and His Friends* (1953). *Neznaika in Sun City* (1958).

Ouspensky, Petr. *In Search of the Miraculous* (1949).

Pelevin, Victor. *Chapaev and Emptiness* (1996). *The Life of Insects* (1993). *The Yellow Arrow* (1993). *Generation "P"* (1999).

Rhinehart, Luke. *Transformation* (1997).

Solo, Vseslav. *Fundamentals of Magic* (1994). *The Temple Gates* (1994).

Strugatsky, Arkady and Boris. *Monday Starts on Saturday* (1965).

Tolkien, J. R. R. *Leaf by Niggle and Other Magical Tales* (1945).

Tsvetkov, Ernest. *Master of Self-Knowledge or Immersion into "I"* (1995). *Psychonomics or the Programmable Mind* (1999).

Volkov, Alexander. *The Wizard of the Emerald City* (1939).

Yogananda, Paramahansa. *Autobiography of a Yogi* (1946).

Zelazny, Roger. *The Chronicles of Amber 1-10* (1970-1991).

Glossary of Russian Personal Names

Feminine (diminutive forms *italicized*)

Anna (*Anya*)
Antonina (*Tonya*)
Anya (Anna)
Dundusa
Elena (*Lena*)
Frosia (Efrosinya)
Galina
Glasha (Glafira)
Irina
Lena (Elena)
Liuba (Liubov)

Liuda (Liudmila)
Liusia (Liudmila)
Manya (Maria)
Maria (*Manya, Masha*)
Marianna
Masha (Maria)
Natalia (*Natasha*)
Natasha (Natalia)
Olga
Polina
Sashka (Alexandra)

Sveta, Svetka (Svetlana)
Svetlana (*Sveta, Svetka*)
Tamara
Tanya (Tatiana)
Tatiana (*Tanya*)
Tonya (Antonina)
Valeria
Varya (Varvara)
Vasilisa
Yulia
Zoya (Zinaida)

Masculine (diminutive forms *italicized*)

Alexander (*Sasha*)
Andrey (*Andriukha*)
Andriukha (Andrey)
Anton
Arkady
Boris
Borisovich (patronymic)
Dima (Dmitry)
Dmitry (*Dima*)
Emelia (Emelian)
Evgeny
Felix
Feodor, Fedor
Gennady
Gregory (*Grisha, Grishka*)
Grisha, Grishka (Gregory)

Ivan (*Vanya, Vanechka*)
Ivanushka (Ivan)
Khron
Kolya, Kolian (Nikolay)
Konstantin
Kozma
Kuzma
Leonid
Martynka (Martyn)
Mikhail (*Misha*)
Misha (Mikhail)
Mitrich (patronymic)
Nikita
Nikolay (*Kolya, Kolian*)
Oleg
Ostap

Pavel
Petr
Porfiry
Sasha (Alexander)
Sergey
Slava
Stepan
Timofey
Vadim
Vanechka (Ivan)
Vasya (Vasily)
Victor
Vladimir
Vseslav
Yan
Yuri

The Luxury of Luck
Editor's afterword

"What are you doing, darling?"
"I'm counting my eyelashes."

Conversation with my young daughter

Even before this book was published, I shared some of its enticing "magical" techniques with a friend. Next time I met her, she dropped her bag to the ground to give me a big hug, and then started telling stories so wonderful I regretted I did not have a voice recorder handy! Here is one of her gems.

One day our cat brought home three kittens, and we drove into town to find them new caretakers. We set ourselves up in a Walmart parking lot, but the prospects of placing three kittens in a small rural community of only 3,000 people were not very bright. After an hour's wait without as much as a single inquiry, my children got bored and told me: "Mama, remember the 'magic' stuff you heard about? Let's try it out!" I liked the idea, and we came up with a terrific story.

We imagined ourselves standing there with our kittens—gray, red, and black—and then a car comes to a screeching halt right in front of us, and the driver asks about the gray one. But before we have a chance to respond, there's a second, then a third car racing over. Before long we are surrounded by a huge crowd, and they all want our kittens!

Some people drove hundreds of miles or even flew in from Europe to adopt a kitten. With a thousand contenders and only three kittens, we end up organizing an auction, and raise so much money that we pay off our mortgage and all our loans, and live happily ever after.

We were really having a good time making it all up and adding ever more details. But no sooner had we finished laughing than a big red pickup truck pulled over. A gentleman lowered the window and asked if he could have a kitten. That same moment an elderly lady leaned out from her car window and exclaimed, addressing the red truck owner: "Which one are you taking? The gray one? Thank God! I want the red one!" I warned her that it had an eye infection (I was sure nobody would want it), but the lady lost none of her enthusiasm: "Oh, I know exactly how to treat eye infections in kittens. In fact, I've been praying for a kitten like this for two weeks now!"

Shortly thereafter the third kitten also found its new home, and we went back to ours, all the while marveling at how wondrous this world is, full of kittens and ladies who pray for weeks to have one!

A veritable avalanche of equally "magical" occurrences made me realize that "luck" is not random coincidence but rather a skill that can be learned. I packed my things and went to Russia to find out more—and what a trip it was! I met some amazing people and was able to confirm that *The Power of Luck* stems from an ancient tradition which few people even know still exists.

There was once a whole guild of *skomorokh*, or itinerant performers, who traveled from place to place giving performances of music, dance, and comedy. It turns out that these performances were not meant to entertain, but rather to teach people *moroka*—a path of transcending difficulties and creating reality through humor. Just imagine teaching it to today's schoolchildren—now *that* would be an education reform capable of changing the world!

It is no surprise that the *skomorokh* were persecuted through the centuries until even the memory of their craft started to fade. At the same time, the understanding of how luck works was lost. Remarkably enough, *luck* comes from the very same root as the Russian word *luch* ("ray") and Latin *lux* ("light"). Being *lucky* (Russian *luchi* = "rays") meant being enlightened, the same way as *luxury* originally referred not to material wealth, but to spiritual light.

Luck is therefore the essence of life itself, and for as long as we are *lucky* to be alive, it pulsates through our veins. The path to being lucky is that of aligning ourselves with the universal flow of light. Entering this flow is easy—it is actually enough to just stop rowing against it! This is why the "soaring" techniques presented in this book work so well and are so... light! After all, it is not so much about *changing* reality as it is about *noticing* all this laughter dissolved in the world around and within us. It is a path of joy and freedom, as innumerable readers of *The Power of Luck* and *The Art of Soaring* by Dolokhov & Gurangov are now experiencing themselves...

As my trip came to its end, I needed to make my way from the uncharted Russian countryside to the airport. This involved walking seven miles on a dirt road to the paved highway, catching a bus into town, and then taking a train to Moscow. As I was walking along that country road looking at the clouds and listening to birds, I heard a car approaching me from behind. I raised my hand and was lucky to get a ride. As it turned out, the woman driving was going all the way to Moscow and was willing to take me along.

We started talking about this and that, and then all of a sudden she cheerfully asked me: "Have you read *The Power of Luck*? It's stunning! It literally saved my life, and I met my new husband through it!" Before I could reply, she told me how she'd been making a very slow recovery after a surgery. One of her girlfriends read *The Power of Luck* and called her up at the hospital, inviting her to a wedding. "Whose wedding is it?" she asked. "Yours!" was the answer. She and her five girlfriends, all unmarried and in their late 40's, arranged a big celebration complete with invitations, limousine, and a dinner at a fancy restaurant. All six brides were wearing white wedding gowns, and even though there were no grooms in sight, everyone had a very good time, and it was certainly a jaw-dropping experience for all the guests. "Guess what? A month after this spectacle I was eating lunch at a cafe and a handsome man asked me if he could have a seat at my table. We've never been apart since—I'm so happy! Actually, all my girlfriends who 'wed' got married that same year!" She then shared more hilarious stories, and we laughed all our way to Moscow.

Many hours later, as I was stepping out of her brand-new white SUV that her husband had given her for her birthday, I caught myself thinking that, amazing as her stories sounded, I no longer felt surprised.

It is just life. A luxurious one.

Leonid Sharashkin, Ph.D.

Ekalaka, Montana
January 1, 2011